"*Raising Good Humans* brings a ⋯ ul parenting. Drawing from her own stru⋯ ⋯enthood, Hunter Clarke-Fields outlines the ⋯ ⋯tep out of stories of *not good enough* and to ⋯ ⋯, and harmonious family relationships."

—**Tara Brach, PhD**, author of *Radical Acceptance*

"*Raising Good Humans* is the guidebook parents need to instill confidence, mental health, and independence in our children while building a durable relationship with them. Written with the compassion, clarity, and truth of someone who's helped families with a variety of issues, *Raising Good Humans* is chock-full of insights, strategies, and exercises for becoming a more mindful parent. Hunter Clarke-Fields is a persuasive evangelist for the power of meditation in our lives and our children's lives. Her book will transform your life for the better—if you embrace the journey. One of the best parenting books I've ever read."

—**Katherine Reynolds Lewis**, author of *The Good News About Bad Behavior*

"*Raising Good Humans* is a loving and honest road map that teaches parents ways to skillfully navigate challenges, as well deepen joy, connection, and love with our children."

—**Shauna Shapiro, PhD**, professor in the department of psychology at Santa Clara University, and author of *Good Morning, I Love You*

"Hunter Clarke-Fields gets it: to raise the children we hope to raise, we have to learn to become the person we hoped to be—and both goals are a journey, not a destination. This wonderful book will help you handle the ride."

—**KJ Dell'Antonia**, author of *How to Be a Happier Parent*, and former editor of *The New York Times' Motherlode* blog

"After reading Hunter Clarke-Fields's fantastic new book, *Raising Good Humans*, I found myself hopeful, if not downright happy, about the future. Young parents are the most important leaders on the planet, and this guide will both inspire and instruct them how to immediately stop raising kids and start leading their babies into good adults."

—**Hal Runkel**, *New York Times* bestselling author of *ScreamFree Parenting*

"*Raising Good Humans* is a clear and direct guide to transforming your relationships with your kids. Rich with touching stories and practical exercises, it shows how healthy parenting stems from your ability to be self-aware and embody what you want most for your kids. Parents everywhere will benefit from Hunter Clarke-Fields's wisdom, humor, and practical guidance in navigating the messy terrain of raising children."

—**Oren Jay Sofer**, author of *Say What You Mean*

"In *Raising Good Humans*, Hunter Clarke-Fields shares her wisdom and personal experience to help parents create peaceful families. Readers will find information and exercises to enhance their ability to ride the rollercoaster of raising kids while maintaining their own sense of emotional equilibrium."

—**Joanna Faber** and **Julie King**, coauthors of *How to Talk So Little Kids Will Listen* and its companion app, Pocket Parent

"One of the most difficult tasks anyone can undertake is having and raising children. In *Raising Good Humans*, Hunter Clarke-Fields instructs and reminds us that children need more than food, clothing, and shelter. She tells us what the 'more' is and how to provide it. Thank you, Hunter."

—**Iyanla Vanzant**, host of *Iyanla: Fix My Life* (OWN)

RAISING GOOD HUMANS

A Mindful Guide to Breaking the
Cycle of Reactive Parenting and
Raising Kind, Confident Kids

Hunter Clarke-Fields, MSAE

New Harbinger Publications, Inc.

Publisher's Note

This publication is designed to provide accurate and authoritative information in regard to the subject matter covered. It is sold with the understanding that the publisher is not engaged in rendering psychological, financial, legal, or other professional services. If expert assistance or counseling is needed, the services of a competent professional should be sought.

New Harbinger Publications is an employee-owned company

NEW HARBINGER PUBLICATIONS is a registered trademark of New Harbinger Publications, Inc.

Distributed in Canada by Raincoast Books

Copyright © 2019 by Hunter Clarke-Fields
    New Harbinger Publications, Inc.
    5674 Shattuck Avenue
    Oakland, CA 94609
    www.newharbinger.com

Cover design by Sara Christian

Acquired by Elizabeth Hollis-Hansen

Edited by Marisa Solís

All Rights Reserved

Library of Congress Cataloging-in-Publication Data on file

Printed in the United States of America

25   24   23

20   19   18   17   16   15   14

For my daughters, who have been amazing teachers, sources of abundant love and joy, and miracles of the universe that I remain in awe of. Thank you.

Contents

Foreword

My early years of parenting were, well, a mess. I was exhausted, irritable, and deeply confused. Yes, I had sweet moments with my daughters, but I was also losing my temper with them. A lot. While other mothers were identifying as Attachment Parents or Tiger Moms, I was apparently subscribing to the Unpredictable and Unhelpful style of parenting. Ugh.

Eventually, I found myself on a journey similar to the one Hunter Clarke-Fields describes early in this book. I inhaled every piece of parenting advice I could find. I read books, signed up for webinars and virtual summits, and made parenting plans that would put high-end event planners to shame. I was going to change.

I did not change.

I didn't realize it at the time, but I didn't need more information. I needed insight and strategies based on those insights. I needed to understand why I was losing my temper and how to stay calm enough to make use of all of the advice I was coming across.

Eventually, I found my way to mindfulness classes.

Don't get me wrong. I was deeply skeptical. I thought mindfulness was a passing fad, no more relevant to my parenting challenges than the drum circles I openly mocked in my college days. As skeptical as I was, though, I was desperate for change and healing and anything that would help me stay calm in rough parenting moments. So I got over myself and gave it a shot.

Over the following months and years, I learned that mindfulness has nothing to do with drum circles or kombucha or clearing my mind.

It was about noticing—noticing what was going on in and around me at any given moment. Rather than judging or freaking out about whatever I found, I learned to get curious about what I noticed. Perhaps most important, I learned how to have compassion for myself in the really hard parenting moments—because, make no mistake about it, no matter how mindful you are, there will always be hard parenting moments.

My mindfulness practice made a huge difference in my parenting experience. The more I meditated, the less reactive I was. The more often I noticed I was about to lose it with my kids, the less likely I was to actually lose it. Instead of berating myself for my mistakes, I reminded myself that parenting is hard for everyone and that it's okay to screw up. I can always begin again.

Once I learned how to calm myself down, I realized that I had an entirely new problem. I had no idea what to say to my kids when I wasn't yelling at them. The truth is that I still wanted them to stop crying or fighting or bickering, but now that I was no longer overriding their meltdown with my own, I was at a loss for words. Once again, I had to dive back into parenting advice to literally learn a new language.

Oh, how I wish Hunter had written *Raising Good Humans* a decade ago.

But here's the thing. She didn't write it back then because she was still on her parenting journey, one that was similar to mine but also uniquely her own, as journeys always are. The fact that Hunter has also lived through the joys and challenges of parenting (and continues to do so even now) is just one of the reasons why *Raising Good Humans* is such a powerful book.

The other reasons all have to do with who Hunter is and what she believes, much of which is encapsulated in my favorite quote from the book: "Want some major personal growth? Six months with a preschooler can be more effective than years alone on a mountain top."

Make no mistake about it, Hunter is serious about the work she does with parents. In her retreats, online trainings, individual coaching, and now in *Raising Good Humans*, Hunter doesn't shy away from encouraging her fellow parents to seek nothing less than major personal growth. She tells us that self-care is not only not optional but that it's actually our "parental responsibility." She pushes us to meditate and deal with our uncomfortable feelings, and seriously consider the role that our parenting choices—from yelling to punishing our children—may be playing in our kids' behavior.

But Hunter doesn't leave us hanging with vague or generic advice. This book is peppered with questions designed to lead readers to their own conclusions and insights, as well as evidence-based practices such as mindfulness and loving-kindness meditations, unhooking from our negative thoughts, the power of saying yes to our experiences, and specific reflective listening practices. And thank goodness for all of this, as it's exactly what so many of us need. (I know I certainly did!)

But a serious call to action isn't the only thing overwhelmed parents need. We also need someone who is going to remind us that as serious as this parenting gig is, we don't need to take it so seriously. I'm so grateful for Hunter's light-hearted tone and compassionate reminders that we don't always have to be working so hard, that we also need to find ways to take it easy and just relax into the moment whenever possible.

The list of insights, suggestions, and possibilities I want to share with you from *Raising Good Humans* is so long that I'd probably end up rewriting the entire book if I got into all of them here. As you dive into *Raising Good Humans*, I encourage you to consider these powerful questions (game changers, really) that Hunter poses in the introduction:

What do you want for your kids? And are you practicing these things in your own life?

If your answer to the second question is anything other than a clear, emphatic *yes*, don't stress. You're in the right place. Whether you're tolerating a tantrum or hanging out alone on a mountain top, Hunter's got the map you need.

—Carla Naumburg, PhD
Author, *How to Stop Losing Your Sh*t
with Your Kids*

Introduction

"When we become parents, we often see ourselves as our children's teachers, but we soon discover that our children are our teachers as well."

—Daniel Siegel and Mary Hartzel

My greatest wins as a mom stem from moments of failure. Allow me to share one of my biggest:

I sat in the upstairs hallway crying. Not gentle crying, but bawling with big, gushing tears—the kind of crying that makes my face look red and puffy. Like I've been in a prize fight. More important, I felt as if I'd been beaten up on the inside. From behind one closed door away, my two-year-old daughter was also crying, because I'd scared her with my anger. The sound of her crying bored into my heart, precipitating another wave of gasping, snotty sobs. I curled up in a ball on the wood floor. I buried my face in my hands.

Who said parenting would feel like this? No one. It's supposed to be filled with soft-focus moments, me gazing lovingly at my child, right? So what is wrong with me?

I was miserable. But after some time I acknowledged to myself that this parenting stuff was H.A.R.D. I slowly sat up with the realization that I'd frightened my innocent toddler. My actions had damaged our relationship. It would have been easy to blame *her* and push through. But I had the presence of mind to realize that I could choose to start over instead.

I wiped my teary, puffy face with my sleeves. My body felt drained and shaky. I took some deep breaths, stood up, and opened the door to offer her comfort.

That day in the upstairs hallway, my journey began.

It would be much easier to tell this story if this were my single big moment of waking up. I wish I could say that right after that I got myself together, vowed to never yell again, and lived happily ever after as a parent. The truth is that I had already lost it too many times to count, and I would mess up many more times after that.

Although I never would've believed it back then, today, with my daughter on the edge of teendom, our relationship is closer than ever. While I certainly get frustrated, I rarely yell at her or her younger sister. My children actually cooperate without threats or punishment (98 percent of the time).

How did that happen? Through my committing to use practical strategies drawn from mindfulness, compassionate communication, and conflict resolution. And that's what this book is all about. In the pages that follow, you'll learn how to go from a stressed parent to a kind and confident one: grounded, calm, and skillful. The tools I've collected here have helped hundreds of other parents build the kind, cooperative relationships they want with their kids.

From those days of near-constant frustration, I went on an epic quest to understand myself and my daughter. I read books, experimented with different practices, attended trainings, and earned certifications in an effort to change my habits. I doubled down on my years of mindfulness study and brought it into my everyday life as a parent. I learned not only how to stop losing my cool but also how to create strong relationships. Now my children cooperate because they *choose* to, not because I threaten them. With this book, I hope to take you on a shortcut—to help you bypass those years of study, training, and trial and error—and give you the eight essential skills that I've found matter most.

The Reality of Parenting

Before Maggie was born, I had a lot of opinions on how to raise kids. I imagined that my child would eagerly do as I asked and not talk back to me. I would be loving but firm, and we would get along. I had visions of us peacefully walking through art museums together (go ahead and laugh).

The reality of toddlerhood hit me hard. Not only did my child not listen to me, she actively resisted nearly every single thing I said. We butted heads daily. My naturally chill husband and I started to see her as a tiny ticking time bomb. Anything could trigger explosive tantrums, with screaming and yelling lasting for (what felt like) hours. My full-time days at home with her left me jumpy and exhausted. *What was wrong with my child? Why??* It wasn't long before I started having my own mommy tantrums too. What a mess!

It's amazing to look back now, see in the photos just how cute she was, and remember how incredibly difficult it was. We shared wonderful, life-altering joy *and* she pushed buttons in me that I didn't even realize I had. At that time, I didn't know that I was reenacting my own father's temper, perpetuating a pattern passed down through the generations.

If you are irritable, frustrated, disillusioned, and feeling guilty—if you are yelling, stomping your feet, or crying—trust me, you are far from alone. When my daughter was little I was irritable, exhausted, ashamed of my anger, and feeling totally guilty.

The day I sat on the hallway floor, I had two choices: I could shame and blame myself, falling into a pit of despair… Or I could accept what was happening and learn from it. So I took my anger and used it as a teacher. I looked at *why* I was getting triggered. I realized that to parent as well as I could, I needed to become calmer and less reactive, and I needed to respond to my daughter with more skillful language, not blameful words that exacerbated the situation.

The good news for you is that if I could turn around my mess of repetitive failures and build strong, loving, connected relationships with my children, *you can too.*

Changing the Perfection Paradigm

It's not easy. As parents, we're given the message that we are always supposed to know what to do. We should be able to effortlessly produce healthy lunches, a tidy home, keep everyone organized, and look great doing it. We *should* have wonderful relationships with our children because the "perfect parent" is always loving, patient, and kind.

But the reality is that sometimes we don't *like* our kids, and sometimes we behave impatiently, yell, and act mean. For most of us, thinking about these missteps brings up a kind of shame that feels unbearable. You can choose to wallow in that, or you can choose to use it as a catalyst to learn and change. I invite you to do the latter.

Modeling in Every Moment

What do we want for our kids? I want my girls to be happy, to feel secure in themselves and confident. I want them to have good relationships with others. More than anything else, I want them to feel comfortable in their own skin—to accept themselves.

What do you want for your kids? After you answer that, the big question becomes, *Are you practicing these things in your own life?*

You've probably realized already that children tend to be terrible at doing what we *say* but great at doing what we *do*. From infancy, we are teaching our children how to treat others by the way we treat them. How we respond to our children on a moment-to-moment basis creates a pattern that our children may follow for a lifetime. Therefore, the onus is on us to behave the way we want our children to behave.

What kind of family life would you like? How do you want to *feel?* Perhaps you want to feel calm. Or you may want to feel less triggered and more confident in your choices. You probably want more cooperation. I invite you to explore your answers to these questions in the following exercise. (It is the first writing prompt of many in this book. I strongly encourage you to dedicate a notebook as your *Raising Good Humans* journal so that you may gather your work in one place.)

Special note: I know how it is, dear reader, when you get to the point in a book when you are asked to do an exercise. You decide that maybe you will do it later and continue reading. However, this is a book that *requires* your participation if you are going to have any meaningful change. Shall we agree this is what we want? Think of this entire book as an exercise in diving into a more rewarding way of parenting, and the following exercise is your first step off the platform. You can do it! Now just go grab a notebook.

Exercise: What's Your Relationship to Your Own Parenting?

It's important to have a clear understanding of how you would like your family life to be day to day, along with what you would like to change to get it there. Take a few moments to contemplate these questions. Write as much as you feel moved to for each one. Date this page in your notebook: it's a snapshot of what your feelings and behaviors are now—and what you want them to be in the future.

How do you feel about parenting now?

What are your frustrations?

What do you want to feel instead?

What would you like to change about your behaviors?

How to Model Conscious Living

This book will help you model calmer, more thoughtful interactions with your child. You'll learn how to communicate skillfully—in ways that make your kids actually *want* to cooperate with you. You'll learn how to take care of your own triggers so that you can show your children how to take care of their big feelings. You'll discover how to live what you want your kids to learn.

You may have seen a parent yelling at a child to be quiet (or you may have had such a moment yourself). Our kids see right through this hypocrisy. If we want our children to learn to be kind and respectful to others (including us), then we must demonstrate kindness and respect. If we want our kids to consider others' needs, then we must show them that we truly consider *their* needs. If we want them to be polite, then we have to consider our own use of courteous words with our children. We must treat our children how we ourselves want to be treated. We should behave as we want them to behave. It's so simple—and not easy at all.

Habits of Disconnection

Unfortunately, as a culture we are in the habit of treating children as less than—and too often we expect behavior of them that we don't really demonstrate ourselves. We expect children to be respectful, yet we continually order them around. We make demands of them, then we are surprised when they are demanding. We yell, threaten, and punish, demonstrating to them that power and coercion are our go-to tools.

Unsurprisingly, this causes disconnection in the relationship. Children start to resent their parents. By the time they are adolescents, they've had it with this kind of treatment and rebel. Then we've lost our influence when our children need it most, during the teen years. Sometimes our relationships remain irreparably harmed into our children's adulthood.

I invite you to consider a better option: You demonstrate the kind and respectful communication you want your child to learn. You be less reactive in the moment and respond to your child more thoughtfully. You get your own needs met and have boundaries, and you communicate these without blaming, shaming, and threatening. You behave as the good human you want your child to be.

Changing Old Patterns

In the pages that follow, you'll learn about harmful patterns that may have been passed down through the generations in your family. As you open your eyes to these generational patterns, let them motivate and teach you.

A few years into working on my own yelling problem, I sat down with my father. He talked to me about the circumstances in which he grew up. His parents beat him with a belt. My grandparents' behavior, which would be called traumatizing abuse today, was then considered normal. My father, in his turn, spanked me.

Now I was on a mission to change things. Not only was I *not* physically punishing my children, I was also trying not to yell. We both saw the improvement down through the generations, but for me, "not yelling" wasn't enough. I wanted to create relationships based on cooperation and respect—and I did so. The old patterns of harshness, anger, and disconnection have been transformed in my family.

No More Threats

You won't find suggestions to use threats or punishment in this book. There are good reasons for this: for one thing, when we threaten our kids, they learn to threaten others. And it's simply a much less effective parenting tool than skillful communication.

Instead, you'll learn tools, grounded in research, that promote everyone's well-being. With a stronger relationship to your child, your influence will grow. It's not magic, and it takes some hard work, but the benefits will last for a lifetime. I've seen this happen time and time again with the students in the Mindful Parenting course that I developed and teach. You can change harmful patterns for generations to come.

When my firstborn was young, we seemed to be in conflict daily. Not only was I terrible at handling her difficult feelings, but my way of communicating made our problems worse. Yet I was able to turn things around using the tools I will teach you in this book. Now we are able to get through conflicts with less frustration and recover from them more quickly. My partner and I have much more cooperation from both children.

A Mindful Path to Raising Good Humans

Most parenting books don't tell you that all their good advice goes out the window when your stress response kicks in—as in, you *literally* can't access the areas of the brain where your good new skills are stored. That's why this book will show you how to quiet your stress response (the reactive, raging banshee inside) and teach you how to communicate with your child effectively (so you stop triggering so much resistance).

Reduced reactivity and effective communication are taught via eight skills that you can implement, even in your busy life, starting right now:

- Mindfulness practices to calm reactivity

- Awareness of your story

- Self-compassion

- Taking care of difficult feelings

- Mindful listening

- Speaking skillfully

- Mindful problem solving

- Supporting your peaceful home

Many parents look at the challenges, irritations, and frustrations of parenting and blame the child. If we can only "fix" our children, life will be better. But instead of blaming your child—or yourself—I invite you to look at the difficulties and stresses of parenting as your teachers—as something to learn from, rather than something you wish would just go away.

This book is divided into two parts. The first half is about the foundational work you can do personally to calm your reactivity. The second half is devoted to skillful communication and cultivating peace in the home. Please don't skip over the initial section of this book! The inner work is the vital foundation for your communication work.

In part I, you will learn the practice of mindfulness to help lessen your stress response and cultivate compassion. Then, you'll become aware of your own story and suss out your triggers. Self-compassion comes next, as the essential attitude for positive change. We conclude the first section with the vital skill of taking care of difficult feelings.

In part II, you'll learn the communication skills that will lead to more cooperation from your child and better relationships. You'll find out how to listen to help your child solve his own problems and improve your relationship. You'll learn how to talk so that you stop triggering so much resistance in your child. You'll discover how to solve problems without resorting to threats so that everyone's needs get met (including yours!). Finally, you'll learn the practices and habits you need to support your new, peaceful home.

I've also created *Raising Good Humans* bonus materials, including guided meditations for parents, that are available for download at the website for this book: http://www.raisinggoodhumansbook.com. I encourage you to visit this site for additional free resources.

I created the Mindful Parenting course out of the struggles in my own life. I was a mom feeling as if I was failing at the most important job in my life. Parenting books had great advice that I couldn't implement because I was so frustrated and stressed. I needed to reestablish my mindfulness practice to get grounded. However, my mindfulness practice didn't help me find the right words to say to my child, words that didn't trigger resistance in her.

Ultimately, this work came together because I realized that one without the other was incomplete. I needed both. The parents I was working with needed both. Mindfulness and skillful communication are the two wings that allow us to fly.

Don't take my word for it. Try it out for yourself. Dedicate this time to not just *reading* about these concepts, but *realizing* them in your own life. That means taking action—writing, practicing, and actually doing the exercises. It also means practicing stillness, which can be scary initially but is ultimately nourishing. You will get out of this what you put into it, so I encourage you to act like a scientist and test these practices in your own life.

I leave you with this Mindful Parenting Manifesto. As you will come to see, this is the guiding light that shines through this book.

Mindful Parenting Manifesto

A Mindful Parent is a new generation of parent: present, evolving, calm, authentic, and free.

Mindful Parents reject the culture of "not good enough," knowing that when we free ourselves from unnecessary stress and limiting stories, our authentic, peaceful nature shines through.

Mindful Parents practice self-compassion and see their challenges as teachers, not flaws.

Mindful Parents value wisdom over reactivity, empathy over obedience, and begin anew every day.

Mindful Parents live what we want our kids to learn, knowing that the best parenting is in modeling.

Mindful Parents go within and get quiet to access their power.

Mindful Parents practice presence, create their experience, embrace imperfection, and love themselves.

Mindful Parents are motivated, knowing that with every step, they are changing things for the generations that follow.

I am a Mindful Parent.

PART I

BREAK THE CYCLE
OF REACTIVITY

CHAPTER 1

Keeping Your Cool

"You can't stop the waves, but you can learn to surf."

—Jon Kabat-Zinn

Imagine that it's 8 a.m. You have a full day ahead, and your child has to be at school at 8:15. The principal has already sent a warning that your child has been late too often. Your little one is taking a lot of time, changing clothes again, and hasn't brushed his teeth yet.

"Honey, hurry up or we'll be late," you call out several times, but your child does not come down. You finally walk into his room to see what's going on, and he throws himself on the floor screaming, "I'm not going to school!"

What did you think as you read this scenario? What did you feel in your body? I can feel my pulse rising, as if my blood is starting to heat up. My jaw feels tight. Feelings of helplessness, anxiety, and frustration all come up. Impatient thoughts run through my mind, my inner voice ranting about the situation.

Here's the important part: all of these reactions *just happen by themselves*. We aren't "choosing" to turn on our frustrated thoughts, helpless feelings, or physiological stress reaction. We react in those moments on *automatic pilot*. Our stress is running the show, dictating our reaction. Our words just fly out. Often, our autopilot script is a replay of the same language our own parents used in those situations.

Wired to React

We are at our worst in the parenting department when we're in reactive mode. Imagine if, instead of that automatic pilot reactivity (and your mom's voice coming out of your mouth), you could respond thoughtfully in those moments? How might that change things?

In this chapter, we'll start by looking at the nervous system and how it can undermine our parenting. Then, you'll learn practices that can help you counteract those tendencies and become less reactive.

What Is the Stress Response?

You can feel it. Your heart beats faster, your blood pressure goes up, and your breathing rate increases under stress. These nearly instantaneous reactions in the body are there to help you fight off the threat or flee to safety. The stress response helped our ancestors survive when they needed to react quickly to threats, because it *literally cuts off our access* to the upper brain (a.k.a. the part that can reason and solve problems), which would only get in the way and slow us down. Ancestral humans wouldn't have made it if they'd paused to be thoughtful about saving their children from a saber-toothed tiger. We needed quick reactions. However, in today's world, these autopilot stress reactions often get us into trouble.

There are biological and evolutionary reasons why we "lose it." In fact, when you look at it from an evolutionary perspective, I would argue that *it's not even your fault* when you lose it. "Losing it" happens when we have automatic reactions because our brain has mistakenly perceived a threat. Conflicts with our kids can trigger these automatic biological reactions. We do not choose to have this response. But, as we'll see, we can choose to temper its effects.

We also don't consciously choose to focus on the problems. Because of this wiring for survival, we all have an innate propensity to be aware of things that could threaten—a *negativity bias*. The lower brain makes sure that we notice the negative more easily, which is helpful in the struggle to survive. However, today the negativity bias can undermine your *connection* to your child—a.k.a. the glue that makes parenting easier. We see our kids' *uncooperative* moments—how about the cooperative ones? We see their selfishness—maybe missing their generosity. Our view of our children can become narrow and biased.

Left unexamined and unchecked, our biology is setting us up for a negative experience of parenting. But it doesn't have to be this way. I will share with you proven tools and practices that will turn things around.

What's Happening Inside the Brain

Let's start by looking at what's happening in the "losing it" brain a little more closely, starting with the stress response in the lower brain. While the whole brain is made up of interconnected networks, it's helpful to think about the deepest parts of the brain—the brain stem and the limbic region—as the areas largely responsible for our stress response, the famous fight, flight, or freeze reaction.

Scientists tell us that these areas of the brain mainly control basic body functions (such as breathing), innate reactions (like fight, flight, or freeze), and strong emotions (such as anger, fear, and disgust). The amygdalae, two almond-shaped clusters in the limbic region, are considered the centers of our threat-detection system. The amygdalae and the limbic system have been honed over millennia to detect and react swiftly to threats, thus keeping us alive. This is so vital that these reactions bypass the upper areas of the brain, which handle the much slower mental processes of thoughtful decision making.

The upper areas of the brain, especially the prefrontal cortex, which lies right behind our foreheads, is generally responsible for complex mental processes including problem-solving, creativity, planning, imagining, and thoughtfulness (Siegel and Bryson 2011). This area is home to the characteristics we need to parent mindfully:

- Rational decision making

- Conscious control over emotions and body

- Self-awareness

- Empathy

Impaired Parenting

Our ability to make thoughtful, deliberate choices depends upon our ability to access the upper parts of the brain, which are the seat of our understanding and empathy. Yet it's exactly that ability that is compromised when we're losing it. Your body's stress response impairs the functioning of the upper brain. The autopilot reactions bypass the prefrontal cortex. This bears repeating: *you literally cannot access the rational part of your brain when your stress response is triggered.*

Losing control isn't a choice that you make. It's your biological system reacting automatically. Therefore, it takes intentional practice to learn to respond differently. It also means that we are not entirely to blame for our own reactivity. Instant reactivity to threat may have been critical for our ancestors. Our amygdalae don't know that we live in a different world today.

That's also why most parenting advice doesn't take hold. Largely, parenting experts neglect to teach us how to take care of our stress response. So, when the going gets tough and we're stressed, we can't access whatever new parenting technique we've learned. Despite the well-meaning good advice that parenting books and blogs offer, it all seems to fly out the window when our stress response kicks in. We're left feeling frustrated. We might even decide we're "bad" parents. But hear me now: There is nothing wrong with you! It is just your biological response—and there are tools to cope with it.

If these ingrained biological processes are responsible, what can be done about it? Happily for you and me, there is a time-tested intervention: *mindfulness meditation.* You may have heard about it from the explosion of press coverage it's received in recent years, but maybe you are not exactly sure what it is. Or you may be thinking, *We're still talking about parenting, right?* Yes, I assure you, we really are.

Mindfulness: The Superpower Parents Need

Mindfulness meditation is the stealth tool that will make all the difference in calming down your reactivity. What is mindfulness? My favorite definition comes from Jon Kabat-Zinn, scientist, author, and meditation teacher who has been influential in bringing mindfulness into the mainstream of medicine and society: Mindfulness is *"the awareness that arises through paying attention on purpose, in the present moment, and nonjudgmentally"* (2018, xxxiv).

As for meditation, it can mean many things to people. For our purposes, it's a practice of training the mind to become less reactive and more present. So mindfulness meditation is intentionally training our attention to be in the present moment, nonreactive, and nonjudgmentally curious. Mindfulness is a quality we are aiming for; mindfulness meditation is the tool for building that quality in ourselves.

Mindfulness meditation has many benefits and effectively zero negative side effects. Researchers from Johns Hopkins University found forty-seven studies that show that mindfulness meditation can help ease psychological stress from anxiety, depression, and chronic pain (Corliss 2014). More research has shown that it increases positive emotion (Davidson, et al. 2002), increases social connection and emotional intelligence, and, importantly, improves your ability to regulate your emotions (this is just what parents need!) (Fredrickson, et al. 2008). I've seen all of these benefits in my own life and in the lives of my clients. Put simply, practicing mindfulness gives us a sense of equanimity and the groundedness we need to parent well.

Mindfulness Meditation Changes the Brain

Mindfulness meditation can significantly change how reactive our brains are over time. We aren't 100 percent sure yet how this happens, but MRI scans show that after an eight-week course of mindfulness practice, the brain's fight-or-flight centers, the amygdalae, actually appear to shrink. Not only that, but as the amygdalae shrink, the prefrontal cortex (again, the area associated with more-complex brain functions such as awareness, concentration, empathy, and decision making) becomes thicker!

What's more, the "functional connectivity" between these regions—how often they are activated together—also changes. The connections between the amygdalae and the rest of the brain weakens, while the connections among areas associated with *attention* and *concentration* get stronger (Ireland 2014). This means that meditation is physically changing the brain (wow!) in a way that weakens our reactivity! This ability of the brain to change is called *neuroplasticity*, and it can happen throughout an individual's life. With mindfulness meditation, our reactive responses to stress can be superseded by more thoughtful ones.

Because of these changes, mindfulness meditation is the foundation we'll develop to help us think more clearly in difficult parenting situations. With reduced reactivity, you'll be able to access the logical, rational, and empathetic prefrontal cortex, allowing you to use the new communication skills you'll learn soon. With some practice in mindfulness meditation under your belt, as well as other practices to lower your stress response, your intention to parent thoughtfully will no longer be hijacked by your reactivity.

> Your child has the same reactive stress response as you have. Her fight-or-flight system will often register a huge, looming parent as a threat. If your child's nervous system sees you as threatening, it will trigger resistance, and she won't be able to learn. This is because the upper parts of the brain (which are less developed in children than in adults) are offline. So when you need to connect with your child, it's important to crouch down to her level and be conscious of how your body and voice might be coming off as threatening. If you make your body seem less threatening, and speak in a calmer voice instead of yelling, you'll have a less-stressed child—and you'll get more cooperation.

Getting off Autopilot

Let's zoom the lens out and look at mindfulness in the bigger picture. We spend most of our time with our children in automatic pilot mode. Our minds are fixed on accomplishing goals, solving problems, planning, and strategizing the day ahead or the next day. In everyday moments with our kids, we are distracted by thoughts of the future (for example, mentally planning dinner while our children are telling us about their day). When we're in that automatic doing/achieving/planning mode, our minds are elsewhere; we're not really in the present moment with our children.

If we're not fully present with our kids, we miss the chance to attune with their cues about what is happening for them under the surface. We might miss the signal that our children need a hug or help instead of more direction in this moment. Without mindfulness practice in our lives, we can make an unskillful choice in that moment—or even become overrun by that powerful stress response. Then, instead of offering our children the thoughtful, empathetic response that might be beneficial in that moment, we're triggered and reactive. We are going to dive deeper into how to disarm these triggers in chapter 2. For now, you'll learn mindfulness practices to help you be less reactive on a moment-to-moment basis.

As we start to practice mindfulness—bringing our attention into the present moment with kindness and curiosity—we can bring that awareness, kindness, and curiosity to our children, bypassing a whole host of problems that arise with distraction. In fact, in my Mindful Mama podcast conversation with Dr. Dan Siegel (2018)—a clinical professor of psychiatry, author, and expert on attachment, mindfulness, and the brain—he said that "parental presence is *key* to optimizing the chance of your child having a life of well-being and resilience."

It sounds amazing, right? But let's be real here: no one is ever going to be 100 percent present. That's totally fine. This is about the middle path: using the tools of mindfulness to reduce our stress response and become more present for our children. We're aiming for "good-enough" parenting.

How to Practice Mindfulness

How do you practice mindfulness? You deliberately focus your attention on what is happening in the here and now, aiming to be *more* attentive to the present moment rather than distracted. You practice noticing what's going on moment to moment, within you and around you, with kindness and curiosity—*nonjudgmentally*. Let's try it now so you can experience exactly what I'm talking about.

Exercise: Mindfully Eating a Raisin

Grab a raisin from your pantry and read these instructions all the way through before beginning. We are going to bring all of our attention and curiosity to this raisin.

Setting Your Intention

Decide to bring all of your attention to this practice, with kindness and curiosity.

Holding

Hold the raisin in the palm of your hand or between your finger and thumb. Focusing on it, imagine that you've just dropped in from Mars and have never seen an object like this before in your life.

Seeing

Take time to really see it; gaze at the raisin with care and full attention. Let your eyes explore every part of it as if you've never seen a raisin before.

Touching

Turn the raisin over between your fingers, feeling its texture. Close your eyes if that enhances your sense of touch.

Smelling

Hold the raisin beneath your nose and inhale the aroma of the raisin. Notice if your mouth or stomach responds as you do this.

Placing

Now slowly bring the raisin up to your lips. Place it in your mouth without chewing. Spend a few moments exploring the sensations of having it in your mouth.

Tasting

Very consciously, take one or two bites into the raisin and notice what happens. Notice any waves of taste as you continue chewing. Without swallowing yet, notice the sensations of taste and texture in your mouth and how these change over time, moment by moment. Notice any changes in the raisin (can we still call this a raisin?) itself.

Swallowing

When you feel ready to swallow, see if you can first detect the intention to swallow as it arises, so that even this is experienced consciously.

Following

Finally, see if you can sense what is left of the raisin moving down into your stomach. Sense how the body as a whole is feeling after completing this exercise in mindful eating.

Welcome to the world of mindful eating! It's just one of the endless number of situations that you can use to practice mindfulness. It's a great way to realize the difference between our normal, distracted, habitual mind and the practice of being fully present.

Start Strengthening Your Nonreactive Muscle

A short meditation practice is the gold standard for reducing your reactivity. Over time, your practice of mindfulness and self-compassion will help you to become less reactive and more accepting of yourself and your child. Most people can expect this to be a bit-by-bit, gradual change. Understanding that daily pressures from family, work, and other commitments consume time and energy, I will teach you mindfulness practices that are short and relate directly to your life, starting with five minutes of sitting mindfulness meditation each day.

Meditation is simply a method of training your attention to reduce stress and reactivity. It's not a religion. It's practiced by people from all walks of life—everyone from CEOs and celebrities to prison inmates. We take care of our bodies with exercise and nourishing food. Meditation is how we take care of our minds. To practice, all you need is your breath.

Choose a regular time each day to establish the habit of sitting meditation. It's lovely to wake up a few minutes early and start your day with a mindfulness practice. It sets the tone for the rest of the day. However, many people practice in the evening, and parents in particular often have to be creative about finding those few minutes. Whether it's morning, lunch break, or nap time, try to find the same time each day. Your goal is to make meditation a habit as regular as brushing your teeth.

Don't skip this foundational work, thinking that you can simply read about it and not actually practice. Just reading about tennis will not make you a better tennis player! The few minutes a day that you dedicate to practicing will help you to become less reactive throughout the rest of the day. Think about it this way: You wouldn't send your child to the final championship soccer game without regular practices. Mindfulness is the same way. You need to practice regularly if you are going to be ready for your equivalent of the big game—your child's tantrum.

Ease your way in, starting with short meditations, then build up to more time, eventually aiming for twenty minutes a day. You can use the guided audio practices from this book's online bonuses at http://www.raisinggood humansbook.com, or you can simply follow the directions below and set a timer.

Practice: Sitting Mindfulness Meditation

Find a quiet time and place. Sit upright but relaxed on a chair or cushion. Be comfortable! You can even meditate in a recliner. Either cup your hands, letting your thumbs touch, or simply rest them in whatever way is comfortable. Set a timer so you don't have to worry about the time.

Close your eyes fully or leave them at half-mast. Bring your attention to your breath and your body. Let your mind be spacious and your heart be kind and soft. Feel your breath at your belly or your nose. Let your breath be natural. Notice each in-breath and each out-breath. Say to yourself, "breathing in" as you breathe in and "breathing out" as you breathe out.

Expect your mind to wander right away. That's normal! The goal is not to stop your thoughts but to train your attention. The goal is to spend more time in the present moment and less time lost in distraction. Label your thoughts "thinking" if you want, then return your attention to your breath. Do this again, and again, and again, and again. Each time you discover that your mind has wandered is an opportunity to do a "rep" and build that mindfulness muscle. Even if you think you are doing this badly, it is still working.

Meditation thrives on practice and a kind approach. If you do this simple practice every day, you will gradually become more grounded and aware.

Your meditation practice can put you back in control of your mind, keeping you from being pushed around by its automatic reactions. It will increase your self-awareness and help you to come back to the present moment rather than be lost in thought. When you can come back to the present and see clearly, many anxieties and fears drop away, and you can be less reactive.

Other Ways to Practice Mindfulness

You'll be able to increase your calm by bringing mindfulness practices into your parenting. They'll help to remind you of the intention to stay calm and to reduce your overall stress levels. You'll start by finding one activity to practice mindfully each day. You'll use this activity as a time to slow down and pay attention with kindness and curiosity.

Practice: Mindful Everyday Activity

We already looked at how to eat mindfully. Now let's use the example of washing dishes, something most of tend to do on autopilot because of how mundane it can be. But doing the dishes can be both satisfying and grounding.

Wash the dishes slowly. Feel the warm water on your hands. Pay attention to the sounds of the plates and cups. Notice the shape of the suds. Let yourself enjoy the experience of making something dirty clean again. When you think about other things, you can acknowledge that your mind has wandered, then refocus on your washing. Focus solely on the doing.

Zen master, mindfulness leader, and peace activist Thich Nhat Hanh explains this task beautifully in his book The Miracle of Mindfulness (1975, p. 85):

> "Wash the dishes relaxingly, as though each bowl is an object of contemplation. Consider each bowl as sacred. Follow your breath to prevent your mind from straying. Do not hurry to get the job over with. Consider washing the dishes the most important thing in life."

What activity will you choose to practice mindfully? Choose one habitual task that you do every day on autopilot. It could be your shower, walking from your car to your office, nursing your child, or whatever is in your routine.

Get Grounded in Your Body

One of the fastest and easiest ways to become present is to practice being mindful of your body. You literally "come to your senses"—feeling what it's like to be alive. When you pay attention to bodily sensations, you're in the here and now. You can't feel yesterday or tomorrow, only right now. The body is a natural anchor for your mindfulness practice.

In challenging parenting moments, paying attention to our body has a grounding effect. When we bring awareness to the body, we're getting down to earth. The body has weight—it offers a good counterbalance to the flighty mind that's constantly zooming off into ideas and ruminations. Mindful of the body, we come into the physical reality of our presence here on earth. And just like other forms of meditation, mindfulness of the body strengthens our attention and reduces stress.

Practice: Get Grounded in Your Body

Follow the simple instructions below, or use the body scan guided meditation at http://www.raisinggoodhumansbook.com. Both approaches will help you get in touch with your body, let go of the to-do list mindset, and release pent-up emotions. The more you practice awareness of your body, the more you'll be able to see and feel the challenging emotions that arise before they build up to anger.

Sit comfortably or lie down. Notice the sensations of touch and pressure where your body meets the surface. Take a deep breath in, noticing how the chest expands. Let that breath out, noticing how the body softens.

Bring your attention into your hands. Can you feel a tingling or vibration there? Let all of your attention focus on the sensations there for a few moments. Be curious about what you feel.

Can you feel a similar sensation in the feet? Throughout the whole body? You may feel pleasant or unpleasant sensations. Try to notice these without judgment, and soften the body with each exhale. Breathe with the sensations in your body for as long as you like.

When you notice the mind wander into thinking, gently let go of those thoughts and come back to feeling your body. When you notice the mind wandering elsewhere (for example, to sounds), acknowledge this also, bring-ing it back to the body, as best you can, with kindness.

Don't worry if you find yourself distracted during the meditation and mindfulness exercises. Unless you are an enlightened master, or dead (!), you should expect the mind to wander—*a lot.* The brain is a thinking machine. When you dedicate yourself to practicing, just a little bit every day, you can get all of the benefits: less stress, less anxiety, less depression, more calm, and a greater sense of well-being.

Plus, far more than toys or lessons, your child needs *you*—the authentic you underneath all of the stress and reactivity—with less tension and more presence and ease. Your ability to be fully present will naturally start to soothe your child, helping him feel seen, heard, and accepted. Thich Nhat Hanh (2003) sums this up wisely:

> *"When you love someone, the best thing you can offer is your presence.
> How can you love if you are not there?"*

Less Autopilot, More Being Present

We don't notice it, but we take a lot of mental shortcuts in family life by using labels. These can be helpful, but labels can also bias us toward seeing a par-ticular thing that we've seen before. For example, if we've labeled one child as the "athletic one," and another as the "smart one," we limit the possibili-ties for these children. It is natural to compare, but sometimes we take our labels too literally. Our preconceived notions about children's behaviors and attitudes get in the way of *really* seeing them.

Since our kids are always changing and labels are static, we must realize that labels can be unreliable. Plus, our preconceived ideas can become a self-fulfilling prophecy—our children live up to our negative expectations. Yikes!

Another way we take shortcuts is with routines. Family life is repetitive: make dinner, clear the table, do the dishes, get ready for bed. Theses routines help us get through life with more ease. The downside is that we can lose our ability to see things with freshness. Often we walk around all day with our heads bent over a screen. We don't appreciate the beautiful sky or the blooming daylilies. What's worse, we miss the sense of curiosity that children naturally bring to the world around them.

Being Open to the Moment and to Change

The truth is that every morning we wake up with a new child. *Every single moment* they are growing, learning, changing. At a biological level, thousands of their cells are dying and thousands are formed in every minute. Children are, quite literally, never the same person twice. Mindfulness helps us to recognize this truth and see our children with fresh eyes in each moment.

At a deeper level, constant change is an undeniable and inescapable fact of human existence. All of us will grow old, get sick, and eventually die. All of our feelings will eventually give way to new emotions. The same holds true for our children's feelings. We suffer when we think of our feelings, behaviors, and thoughts as "always" and "never."

Think about this: what's at the root of your fear when you've discovered that your child has lied (again)? Most likely you fear that your child will *always* be this way, destroying your relationship forever and ruining her chances of a successful and happy life. "Always" thinking leads us down a scary rabbit hole of anxiety. Without the thought, *My child will always be like this*, you'd be in a much more grounded and calmer state to deal with the *actual* situation.

Plus, when we remember the truth of constant change in our daily lives, it's easier to feel gratitude for what we have in the present moment, because nothing lasts forever. We don't. Our children don't. Our problems don't. There are a lot of good reasons to practice to become fully present for life now.

Being present means really seeing, hearing, and understanding your child. It means letting go of your agenda and preconceived notions to instead be curious about what is. Your meditation practice will help you become more present for your child. But you will need more than that. The next few practices will help you deepen your awareness to the present moment.

Beginner's Mind—Learn from Every Moment

What if we could see our moments with our children with fresh eyes? We can, and it's called *beginner's mind*. This Zen Buddhist practice can help us calm our reactivity, seeing life as a beginner, as if every situation is a learning opportunity.

When we slow down and live more mindfully—with awareness of the present moment nonjudgmentally—we see the richness of the world around us. Savoring and appreciating the world not only feels good, it also lowers our stress and helps us see problems more clearly (and less judgmentally). When we practice beginner's mind, we can see the world as it is, rather than our old ideas of how we *think* it is.

Consider beginner's mind as a practice of trying to see each new experience as exactly that—a *new* experience. Think of it as bringing a "freshness" to each moment. Try the following practices this week. They will help you get out of autopilot mode, let go of preconceived notions, and move into a place of presence and curiosity. And remember, *what you practice grows stronger.*

Practice: Beginner's Mind on a Walk

Start by seeing the activity of walking with fresh eyes, as if you don't know what to expect, as if you haven't done it thousands of times already.

Really look at the path, the trees or concrete, the buildings and landscape. Try to see the details that you might not normally notice.

Notice the textures, tastes, smells, and appearance of the world around you. Pay close attention, as if you don't already know where your walk will take you.

Practice: See Your Child with Fresh Eyes

Imagine that you're meeting your child for the first time. See him with fresh eyes, curious about who he is, as if you haven't known him all of his life.

Really look at your child: his hair, his smile, his clothes and shoes, the way he moves his body. Be curious. Try to see details you might not normally notice.

With an attitude of curiosity rather than judgment, notice the way your child interacts with others. Pay close attention and allow yourself to be surprised.

With a regular practice of beginner's mind, it will become easier to see your child as she is *now*—rather than your image of who she was in the past. With this attitude, you don't limit your child's possibilities (or your own) with labels. You can see her more fully and openly.

Acknowledgment—Say What You See

We can intentionally practice mindfulness in our lives with children using the tool of mental and verbal *acknowledgment*—accepting and identifying what is happening in our present moments. In the following section, I'll show you how we often miss this step, and how we can use it with our children, ourselves, and our meditation practice.

Mindful Acknowledgment with Children

I see this scene often: a child comes to a parent visibly upset. The parent wants to make the child feel better, so he skips right to trying to fix her problem. It usually sounds like, "Why don't we...," or "You can just _____ instead." A solution is offered and the problem is solved...right?

Yet with this response, parents have just missed a potent opportunity to connect. They've skipped over the powerful step of acknowledgment—recognizing what's happening for the child in that moment. Acknowledgment shows that we are seeing and accepting the truth or existence of something, such as the child's hurt feelings.

Acknowledging can be magic with our children. They have a great need for us to recognize their thoughts and feelings—to *really hear and see* them. As parents, we often want to skip over this step and solve their problems. Instead, when we say what we see, our children feel seen and heard, which makes nearly every situation better.

Karen's Story

Four-year-old Asher was having a blast playing when it was time to go. He did not want to leave, but he had a doctor's appointment. His mom, Karen, remembered the skill of acknowledgment as Asher began to protest. Karen said to Asher what she was seeing: "You really don't want to go. You wish you could stay. I get it. We've got to go, though." Asher wasn't thrilled about it, but he left with less fuss than usual. He felt seen and heard. His feelings were respected. Acknowledgment means "I see you."

Our Acknowledgment Pressure Valve

Acknowledging our feelings is a mindful way of deflating the drama bubble. Feeling irritated with your kids? Say what you see out loud: "I'm feeling grumpy right now." Simply acknowledging that can provide a lot of relief, and it communicates to your child what's going on with you. Win-win! You're feeling slightly better and you've modeled healthy emotional intelligence for your child.

Anger is often the result of other feelings that have escalated to exasperation (we'll talk about this more in the next chapter). By practicing acknowledgment, you can sometimes head anger off at the pass. When I honestly say to my daughter, "I'm feeling really annoyed right now," it provides relief for my pent-up feelings and lets us back off and allow some space.

Yet, we usually try to hold in anger. What does stuffing our feelings do to us? Picture pushing an inflatable beach ball under the water: sooner or later, it pops out with even more energy than before. Instead, practice saying what you see. When you do, you're bringing the verbal prefrontal cortex online and relieving the pressure of built-up feelings.

Acknowledgment in Meditation

Mindfulness meditation invites us to acknowledge our thoughts, feelings, and sensations in the present moment. Do this in meditation by bringing your attention to each moment as it comes rather than imposing ideas about how it *should* be. If you are stressed and irritable, acknowledge that, and allow those feelings to be there. If you are physically uncomfortable, acknowledge that truth, rather than try to deny it and suffer through. If you are thinking about the future during your meditation practice, acknowledge that.

How does this look in actual practice? Just *mentally say what you see*. In meditation, this is called *noting*. During my meditation, I often find myself mentally planning events for the day to come, so I internally note "planning." If you find that you are feeling jumpy? Mentally note "agitated."

Practice this in both your meditation and in daily living to experience the relief that comes from acknowledgment. The following exercise sums up how to do it in everyday life.

Practice: Acknowledgment

During the next several days, practice saying what you see for both yourself and your child. This brings you into the present moment and acknowledges what is actually happening.

1. *To note internal feelings, look inside. Say what you see. Are you feeling grumpy? Tired? Say, "I'm feeling grumpy right now."*

2. *To note what is going on with your child, say what you see. Verbally acknowledge your child's feelings. Say, "You're upset that it's time to stop. You wish you didn't have to go to bed."*

As you practice acknowledgment, start to notice how you feel and how others respond. Jot down your observations in your Raising Good Humans *journal. As you see positive changes, your new habit will be bolstered.*

Acknowledgment of Negative Thoughts

Acknowledging can also help us get some perspective on thoughts that may trouble us outside of meditation. Our thoughts are mental words or pictures that grab our attention. These thoughts may or may not be true, and often, they pull our attention from the present, where life is meaningful. Negative thoughts, such as *I'm a terrible parent*, can hook us, leaving us caught up in a net of negativity.

Instead of letting these thoughts rule you, you can interrupt them and unhook from the thought. How do you do that? Put the phrase "I'm having a thought that…" in front of your negative thought. This acknowledging gives you a bit of space from an unhelpful thought so that you can choose to pay attention to the present moment.

Practice: Unhooking from Negative Thoughts

Thoughts such as I'm not good enough and I'm a terrible parent and more can hook your attention and distract you from being present with your child. Negative thoughts also prevent you from making good choices. You can take your mindfulness into daily life by interrupting these unhelpful thoughts with acknowledgment. Follow these steps:

1. *Notice when you are getting tight, constricted, irritated, or sad. Then notice if there is a thought behind the sensation or feeling, such as "I'm terrible at this" or "There's something wrong with my child."*

2. *Mentally put the phrase "I'm having a thought that…" in front of the unhelpful thought. For example, "I'm having a thought that I'm not doing enough for my child."*

3. *Breathe. Then choose your next action from a place of clarity.*

Unhooking from negative thoughts doesn't mean that they will go away forever. Our minds will continue to tell us stories. However, unhooking from these thoughts can help us choose our actions with more intention.

Getting caught up in negative thoughts can prevent you from doing things that are important to you, like paying attention to your child. Make unhooking from these unhelpful thoughts a regular practice.

Awareness and acknowledgment can become powerful ways to shift the culture of your home. Cultivate the habit of saying what you see. Start to recognize what is really happening—for your child, for your feelings, and in your meditation practice—and a true sense of clarity will follow. Mindfulness gives us the *space* to be able to *choose* what to say next.

A Foundation for Less-Reactive Parenting

Our reactive moments are when we are at our parenting worst. When the stress response bypasses the rational and empathetic parts of the brain, unskillful orders, threats, and yelling come out of our mouths, pushing our children away and making them *less* likely to cooperate with us in the long run.

While our wiring to react may be helpful in emergency situations, most of the time we are far more effective, thoughtful parents when we can calm down our stress response. Mindfulness meditation is a research-proven way of building that nonreactive muscle, bit by bit, over time. That's why it's a foundational skill. It will give you clearer thinking in every area of your life. You don't have to be perfect at mindfulness and beginner's mind practices, but notice how these skills can shift your experience as a parent.

In the next chapter, we are going to dive deeper into self-awareness to look at the way we were parented and the stories that shape the way we parent now. You'll learn to see the things that trigger your reactivity and acquire tools to help you calm down when things get hot.

For now, make this more than just an intellectual exercise by practicing. You can do it!

What to Practice this Week

- Mindfully Eating a Raisin
- Sitting Mindfulness Meditation for five to ten minutes, four to six days per week
- Mindful Everyday Activity
- Beginner's Mind practice
- Acknowledgment practice
- Unhooking from Negative Thoughts

CHAPTER 2

Disarming Your Triggers

"The best predictor of a child's well-being is the parent's self-understanding."

—Daniel Siegel

There are probably a lot of wonderful things about your parents that you want to pass down to your child: creativity and encouragement, open and honest discussions, and your mom's special pancake recipe. Reactivity? Explosive anger? Um, no.

Once you establish a steady meditation practice, you can expect your reactivity to reduce over time. It's certainly helped with my explosive anger problem. But you can do more to help excavate your inner Zen Mama or Zen Papa. In this chapter, I'm going to share an exercise that will help you understand *why* you're triggered. On a practical basis, we're also going to talk about how to yell less. And you'll learn more practices to help you chill out and become less reactive during heated moments.

Kids Bring Up Our Stuff

The early years of parenthood can make us feel as if we've totally lost our marbles. We are under intense psychological strain. We're back in the parent-child relationship, and it's hard to recognize how much baggage we're bringing from the past.

When my daughter didn't listen, it brought up unresolved issues around not feeling heard. But at the time, I had no idea this was going on. Anger would well up like I hadn't felt since I was…a child. Before I did the excavation work to understand what was triggering me, I blamed my daughter. What's wrong with *her*? Why won't she listen to me? It was clearly all her problem. If I could fix *her* behavior, then everything would be better. Right?

Like little spiritual masters, children have an uncanny ability to reveal our unresolved issues. Something about your parenting experience driving you bananas? That's your inner work. Want some major personal growth? Six months with a preschooler can be more effective than years alone on a mountaintop. It might just be the fast track to enlightenment.

All snark aside, it can be truly helpful to see our times of parental difficulty and challenge as opportunities to heal old wounds. As we heal our inner hurts, we can show up with more presence for our children, allowing us to be a comforting presence for them when they are hurting. Healing old wounds also helps us to hold our firm boundaries with compassion.

We began this chapter with a quote from Dr. Dan Siegel: "The best predictor of a child's well-being is the parent's self-understanding." What this means is that when we understand *why* we are so reactive—what old patterns and wounds are being triggered for us—we can begin to heal and choose a different way of being, rather than repeating dysfunctional family patterns. We can have a chance to refrain from unwittingly passing this baggage onto our kids.

Dan Siegel and Mary Hartzell explain this concept beautifully in *Parenting from the Inside Out* (2004, 18):

> *The intrusions of unresolved issues can directly influence how we know ourselves and interact with our children. When unresolved issues are writing our life story…we are no longer making thoughtful choices about how we want to parent our children, but rather are reacting on the basis of experiences from the past… We often try to control our children's feelings and behavior when actually it is our own internal experience that is triggering our upset feelings about their behavior.*

I bet you remember plenty of moments when your child said or did something that triggered an outsized reaction from you, a time when your internal response seemed out of proportion. I've had many of these moments. We all have them.

Seeing Your Issues Clearly

Understanding why you are triggered will help you respond more thoughtfully. *Without awareness,* you react out of old conditioning—that's when your mom or dad's voice flies out of your mouth. So if, for example, you are aware that you were raised to believe that little girls should always look clean and pretty, you'll understand why your brain is freaking out when your daughter walks barefoot through the mud and gleefully streaks it all over her face. Knowing that this discomfort is *your* stuff and not hers, you can practice some restraint (deep, slow breaths!) and interrupt any old, harmful patterns of shaming and blaming your child.

With your meditation practice and the work you'll do in this chapter, you'll start to understand when you are present and responding thoughtfully, and when you are reacting out of old conditioning. You're going to boost your self-awareness, which will absolutely make parenting easier in the long run. Knowing that your reactions come from you own stuff can help you step back a bit in many parenting situations. Rather than screaming about the spilled juice, we can sigh it out, take deep breaths, or even walk away for a moment to regain some equilibrium. Remember, however, we all parent partially *with* awareness and partially *without*—and that's fine. Your goal is to simply increase your self-awareness bit by bit, day by day. Don't expect to transform into an enlightened, perfect parent.

Sam's Story

Sam was taking some time off from her work as a university admissions counselor to stay at home with her two-year-old daughter and her baby boy. One afternoon, she had just cleaned the house when her daughter spilled orange juice all over the kitchen floor. Sam lost it. She kept thinking, "I can't believe I just spent money and time cleaning this house! She's not even apologizing for it!"

Working through the exercise below, she discovered that wounds from the past were driving many of her feelings and actions. Her trigger? Perfectionism. Sam had been brought up to believe that physical appearance was very important. She realized how outsized her reaction was for a toddler's spill. By looking back at how she was raised, Sam could see that her anger was coming from her own conditioning.

Sam also discovered an old wound around not being heard, when her daughter didn't listen to her right away. She realized that she felt overlooked, not seen. By taking time to uncover these issues, she remembered her family constantly telling her not to be "so sensitive" and to "toughen up." Her feelings drove her to react with more aggression and irritation than the situation warranted. She knew if these issues remained unconscious and unresolved, she would just pass on her baggage to her daughter.

If we never look at our old wounds and triggers, we'll continue to respond out of habit from the past and probably pass down our hurts to our children. Becoming conscious of these wounds will allow us to carry our own baggage rather than passing it down the generational line. Think of this as an opportunity to heal wounds not only for yourself but for generations to come.

Looking Back at Your Childhood

You don't have to repeat the patterns of your parents and grandparents. Examining your own childhood can help you move beyond the limitations of your past. While you may look back and find many positive seeds that you want to pass on to your children, you may have had a difficult childhood. There may be hurts and difficulties that have become the catalyst for your reactivity—but also for the strength and resiliency that you have now. A deeper self-awareness gives you greater compassion toward yourself and others—and can give you the possibility of choosing new ways of being rather than blindly repeating the past.

Ready? The following exercise will help you start to understand how your experience of childhood affected you. Don't be tempted to skip this! You may think, *I've thought about my childhood plenty. I don't need this.* That would be a mistake, because the clarity you can gain by exploring the past will lead to you learning new things about yourself.

Exercise: How Were You Parented?

Writing down your answers to these questions *will* clarify your understanding of your behaviors in a way that will help you see clearly what you are bringing to the relationship with your child. This can be deep and emotional work. Allow yourself time to digest this information—go for a walk, sleep on it—then write your takeaways from this exercise. It's also a great idea to talk about what you've written with a trusted friend or therapist.

Who was in your family and what was it like growing up with them?

How did you get along with your parents when you were little? How did your relationship shift over time?

Did you ever feel rejected or threatened by your parents? Were there experiences that felt distressing during your childhood? Do these experiences continue to influence your life?

How did your parents discipline you as a child? How did you respond to that when you were young? How do you feel it affects your role as a parent now?

Do you recall your earliest separations from your parents? What were they like? Did you have any prolonged separations from your parents?

How did your parents respond to you when you were distressed or made mistakes? How did it make you feel? What kind of language did your parents use? How did they respond when you were happy or excited?

How have your childhood experiences influenced your relationships as an adult? Do you find yourself trying not to behave in certain ways because of what happened to you as a child? Do you have patterns of behavior that you'd like to change?

What impact do you think your childhood has had on your adult life in general, including the ways in which you think about yourself and the ways you relate to your child? What would you like to change about the way you understand yourself and relate to others?

Above all, I want you to remember this: as you learn more about yourself and become more aware of past or present shortcomings, it doesn't help to shame or blame yourself. Cultivate an attitude of kindness and compassion toward yourself throughout the learning process.

The insight you gain from answering these questions, reflecting on your answers, and possibly sharing them with someone you trust will help you see what you are bringing to the table. Don't despair if it feels like a lot of issues! Although the events of our childhoods made little sense at the time, it is possible to make sense of them as adults and understand how they influence us. Resolving our past hurts sometimes means that we have to face the difficult feelings that come along with them.

As you work through the questions above, feel free to jump to chapter 4, where I'll give you more tools to take care of difficult feelings. You may want to get closure on an old hurt by writing a letter. Chapter 7 has the template for a "Letter of Beginning Anew," which can be truly healing.

When you are ready to look at these issues and understand how they are affecting your life, you are already on the path to healing and growth. In the next section, we'll look at the ways we currently respond to those tough parenting moments.

Tame Your Triggers

When my daughter was hovering around two years old and my anger arose, I felt terribly guilty. What was wrong with me for being angry at this innocent child? Like many of us, I had been conditioned to believe that anger was bad, and that (particularly as a woman) I *shouldn't* feel anger like that. In reality, it's a shame how often we deride ourselves and each other for having strong feelings. It's like berating someone for breathing. We can't be living, breathing human beings and not feel emotions, including the difficult ones like anger. Babies, other mammals, and even reptiles feel anger! So instead of vilifying yourself for feeling anger, let's understand it.

Understanding Anger's Fire

Anger is one of our most powerful emotions, and its inward and outward effects can be disastrous. When we look through the lens of evolution, we can see that its function is to help us remove obstacles that thwart us. It tells us, "Something needs to change in this situation!" Anger is a strong motivator for action and change, which can be beneficial.

An interesting feature of anger is that it can hold us in its grip for a while. It comes with a *refractory period*—when all the information we take in confirms or justifies the emotion we're feeling. This is how we become "blinded" by emotion over a period of minutes or even hours. The energy of anger is usually directed outward, which drives us to blame, act aggressively, punish, and retaliate. We exaggerate all the negative qualities of the person who is the target of our anger and become blind to any positive aspects (Cullen and Pons 2016).

Anger is often called a secondary or "iceberg" emotion because underneath it is often a host of other feelings that are driving it: fear, sadness, embarrassment, rejection, criticism, stress, exhaustion, irritation, and more. Thus, when your child behaves wildly in a public place, embarrassment can set off your anger and trigger a response that perpetuates a pattern passed down in your family through generations.

It's important to understand that ideas and beliefs—ingrained in us in childhood—can trigger our anger. Culturally sanctioned ideas, such as "Kids should obey their parents" and "If children respect you they will listen," might cause you major discomfort in many parenting situations, yet you may not even be aware of it. The "How Were You Parented?" questions, presented earlier in this chapter, can help uncover some of these unconscious scripts. Your mindfulness meditation practice will also increase your overall awareness of your thoughts—including subconscious thoughts like these that may be underlying your anger.

Yelling: A Solution That's Actually a Problem

When we get overwhelmed and angry at our kids, most of us find ourselves yelling—especially if a parent yelled and shouted to control the situation and dominate us when we were children. However, it rarely solves the situation. Yelling may quiet children and make them obedient temporarily, but it won't correct their behavior or their attitudes in the long run.

Almost immediately, yelling triggers the fear center in children's brains, causing the same stress response that we looked at in ourselves in the previous chapter. Yelling rings the limbic system alarm bell, causing kids to be alert and self-protective. Instead of learning from the moment, their stress response bypasses the upper parts of the brain and causes children to fight back, talk back, withdraw, or run away. *They are not "misbehaving" in these moments, they are experiencing a stress response.*

Because of their stress response, children can't sit still, pay attention, or learn. In a moment when we want our children to learn to change their behavior, yelling is actively counterproductive. Furthermore, research has shown that yelling makes children more aggressive physically and verbally (Gershoff, et al. 2010). So the effects on their behavior are bad in both the short and the long term.

Yelling also erodes our relationship with our children. Because children's cooperation is fueled by our close, connected relationships, yelling undermines our ability to successfully guide our children to more skillful choices. When we yell a lot, our children may gradually come to resent us. They may start yelling back—at us, or at their peers and siblings—because they think that yelling is how to get what you want: we've modeled this for them. Also, sadly, children sometimes think that their parents who yell don't love them, setting them up for a lifetime of limited self-esteem.

All that said, please don't worry—it's unlikely that you have damaged your child by yelling. All of us yell sometimes, and we'll continue to do so from time to time because we're human. As you become more aware of the problems with yelling, I invite you to make your goal to yell *less*. Your mindfulness meditation practice will help you do that as you work at nonreactivity. Remember, what you practice grows stronger.

Identify Your Triggers

As we talked about in the previous chapter, we (and our nervous system) are products of thousands of generations of humans who evolved to be aware of threats. We didn't choose our nervous system's response to challenging situations (for example, we don't usually choose to yell). Furthermore, events in our early childhood *that we may not even remember* could trigger an emotional response that swamps our rational brain's ability to override our limbic system.

Our responses to emotions can be functional as well as dysfunctional. If we experience anger and use our energy to organize a group dedicated to social action, our response is extremely functional. If we hurt ourselves or others, we're on the dysfunctional side of anger—and dealing with a response that might be triggered by an imported script from a past trauma.

It helps to understand why we are triggered. What are those "buttons" that your children push? In the following exercise, I invite you to consider what triggers your anger and how you habitually respond.

Exercise: Triggers and Reactions

What triggers your anger? In your journal, make a list of your most sensitive triggers.

Common Triggers

- Feeling misunderstood or contradicted

- Lacking control in a situation

- Feeling that someone is upset with you

- Feeling disrespected or that an injustice occurred

- Being excluded

- Tiredness, physical discomfort

What are your frequent reactions to anger? List your most common reactions.

Common Reactions

- Blame and/or resentment

- Sadness and lethargy

- Checking out of a tense situation

- Sarcastic or passive-aggressive comments

- Insulting the other person

- Avoiding eye contact

- Constructing a story about disagreeable situations

- Interrupting others

Once you have identified your common triggers and reactions, start to notice how they arise in everyday life. When we realize in the midst of a difficult situation that the "lacking in control" trigger is coming up, for example, we're already interrupting the usual autopilot reaction.

Becoming aware of the inner experience of your triggers and anger can help you catch it sooner. We're going to take this awareness of your reactions a step further in the next exercise.

Track Your Triggers

I invite you to take a full week to track every time you yell or feel like yelling. The goal at first is not to change your actions but to understand where they are coming from. What are the situations that set you off? Why does that situation trigger your stress response? All the information you collect in your journal will provide insight into changes you can make in your routines, self-care, and environment that will help you yell less.

Sheila McCraith has great advice for tracking your triggers in her book *Yell Less Love More* (2014). She reminds us to be detailed, truthful, and committed—and to stick with the practice of tracking even if you feel as if you have enough information. The point of tracking your triggers is to see patterns and trends. Awareness is the vital foundation for making change.

Exercise: Keep Track of Your Triggers

Take a week to track every time you yell or feel like yelling. You may want to write out each occurrence, or you can make a chart. Keep it in a handy place so that you can gather the information right away.

Information to Track

1. Person you yelled at

2. What happened (surface trigger)

3. How you felt (deeper trigger)

4. Whether anyone was tired or hungry

What you could have done differently

It can be discouraging to realize how often you yell. As you go through this exercise, I want you to remember that you are far from alone—strong emotions are part of being human. No one expects you to be perfect, and your kids do not need you to be perfect. In fact, as you make mistakes and try again, your child will be learning from you how to grow and be resilient.

How to Yell Less

When my sleep was being interrupted at night, I was on the brink of losing it almost every day. My cup was near empty, so when I dug deep for resources to deal with my child's tantrums in a more empathetic way, there was nothing there. When we're not meeting our own needs, we have nothing to give.

Reduce Your Overall Stress

Reducing our overall level of stress might be the *number one most effective thing we can do to yell less.* When we are not getting enough sleep, when we have committed to too many responsibilities, when we are constantly rushing to tick things off our to-do lists, when we have negative self-talk, we are much more likely to lose it with our kids.

This is one of the reasons why the "self-sacrificing parent" idea is so insidious. When we constantly sacrifice our own needs in favor of our children's, we all lose. Our children lose out by having an ungrounded parent who is frequently on the brink of collapse. We lose out on enjoying our life and our children. We also perpetuate this harmful pattern—effectively passing the buck to the next generation.

Does any of this ring uncomfortably close to truth for you? If so, I invite you to journal on where your belief that "good parents sacrifice themselves for their children" comes from. As you start to bring more awareness to this (often subconscious) belief, you can interrupt the pattern and make new choices.

I want you to realize that self-care is not selfish. On the contrary, *it's your parental responsibility.* It's time to take responsibility for the stress levels in your life and make some choices to reduce your overall stress.

Whole books have been written about stress reduction, but for now, here are my top three most important things to do (aside from mindfulness meditation) to lower your overall stress levels:

- **Exercise regularly.** Exercise is vital for you physically and mentally. It provides an outlet for stress and helps your body release endorphins, which increase your feelings of overall well-being. Find a way to get your sweat on that's fun for you.

- **Get enough sleep.** Lack of sleep can negatively impact every single thing you do as well as every relationship. There are many things you can do to improve your sleep habits, from using time management strategies to carve out more time to finding relaxation techniques to help you fall asleep and get quality rest all night.

- **Spend time with friends and family.** Social support can keep you healthier and happier, creating a buffer against stress. Friends can pick you up when you're sad, provide insights when you're confused, and help you have fun when you need to blow off steam. Prioritize time with your loved ones.

Your regular mindfulness meditation practice will reduce your stress. It will also serve you in your non-meditation moments by helping you to interrupt *rumination*—the habit of going over and over thoughts that induce anxiety—and become more present. You can do your short meditation multiple times a day to help reduce stress, or try it before bedtime to help you sleep.

Meeting your own needs for sleep, exercise, meditation, and time with friends is essential to living a happier life as a parent. Plus, you are modeling how to live life for your child. Yes, your own needs can be postponed sometimes, while an infant's can't. But not indefinitely. You are living what you want your kid to learn. Is your child learning how to take care of herself and her needs in a healthy way, or is she learning a lack of self-regard and self-worth? Which do you want for your child?

Cool the Flames When Things Get Hot

Mindfulness meditation and reducing your overall stress will help reduce your tendency to get triggered, but there will inevitably be times when you lose it. What do you do in those moments?

Anger is tricky because there are costs to both showing your anger and suppressing it. Suppressing it only postpones the problem while it quietly simmers under the surface, wreaking havoc on your body. But if we express it, we risk hurting those we love. What do we do? Happily, there is a third path.

Anger is an energy that needs to move through our body, so we can mindfully notice the feeling arise and let the energy of anger move through us. I like to call this "taking care of" our anger: we release the energy of anger and calm down our nervous system.

We will practice restraining that autopilot reactivity in favor of some new responses. These responses don't take much time—sometimes only a few seconds and at least the same amount of time as yelling—but your new response will be like a muscle that you have to build. Responding in a new way may be hard at first, but the payoff in increased connection with and cooperation from your child are more than worth it.

Step Away

When you're about to lose it, the nervous system perceives a threat or an obstacle. So you must let your body and mind know that you are *safe* in the moment. One way to do that is by stepping away from the scene. As long as your child is safe, it is far better to go to the next room than to scream at your child.

When my daughter was young enough to still be in a crib, I was on the verge of exploding when she wasn't listening to me. I would put her in that crib, walk out of her room and onto my bedroom balcony, and close the door to breathe and calm down. Walking away when you're about to lose it is a skillful choice.

Talk Yourself Down

We can let the nervous system know that we're safe by telling ourselves, *This is not an emergency. I can handle this.* Saying these words helps to bring the verbal prefrontal cortex back online and slows down that stress response. You can try saying, "I'm helping my child," to remind your nervous system that your child is not a threat. These are ways to use the power of thinking to calm down the body.

Shake It Out

Remember how the stress response is responsible for building up your blood pressure, making your muscles tense, and preparing your physiological system to fight? Well, when you're angry, the anger has built up an excess of energy in your system that you *need* to release. Don't be tempted to punch a pillow or yell—what you practice grows stronger.

Instead, try shaking it out—literally shaking your hands, arms, legs, and whole body to release the energy. Many animals are known to shake dozens of times a day to clear away the effects of stress. Young children know this and naturally shake and wiggle away their tension. You'll look silly but feel good. Actually, it's a lovely bonus when you can laugh at yourself—laughter is the antithesis of anger!

Strike a Pose

Yoga provides effective body and breath practices to calm down the nervous system. A simple way to release the energy is to do a forward fold, which is calming and cooling: from standing and with knees slightly bent, slump over like a ragdoll. Or get grounded in child's pose: from kneeling, with feet together and knees wide, fold forward, resting your forehead on the floor and your arms stretched out either in front of you or at your sides. These poses cut off our outward engagement to help us focus inward. Letting out a few cleansing sighs can be an effective release of tension.

Breathe

"Take a deep breath" is cliché because it's true. With deep breathing, you are increasing the amount of oxygen in the body, showing the nervous system that everything's "okay," and slowing your heart's pace, creating feelings of calmness and relaxation.

Practice: Breathe to Release Tension

There are many breathing techniques out there. Here are two that can move you away from the stress response and into the opposite: rest and relaxation. Practice these deep breathing exercises to release tension at any time in your day, so that it's easier to remember them in difficult moments!

Three-Part Breathing

This breath, also called "complete breath," helps induce feelings of calmness and relaxation. Each in-breath and out-breath is divided into three parts with a very brief pause between them.

1. *Breathe in slowly through the nose, sending air to the bottom of the lungs (fill the abdomen). Pause.*

2. *Then, sip in more air to fill up the ribcage. Pause.*

3. *Next, fill up the chest to your collarbones. Pause.*

4. *Breathing out through the nose, relax the chest and let out the air below the collarbones naturally. Pause.*

5. *Then, relax the ribcage, releasing more air. Pause.*

6. *Finally, pull in the belly to release the rest of the air and complete the exhale.*

7. *Repeat four times or as much as needed.*

Five-Eight Breathing

Counting the breath forces the mind to focus on the present moment, moving attention away from the perceived stressors. This deep breath helps calm the body.

1. *Count slowly to five while taking a deep breath in through the nose.*

2. *Exhale out of the nose or mouth slowly so that it takes a full count of eight to completely exhale.*

3. *Repeat four times or as much as needed.*

Create Your Unique Plan

Our responses to difficult parenting moments are as varied as ourselves and our personal stories. You may have grown up with a parent who withdrew or became passive-aggressive when angry. Or you might be playing out the generational pattern of the adult temper tantrum, yelling like I did. Because our experiences are so varied, there's no perfect one-size-fits-all solution to yelling less.

In the next exercise, you'll find a set of tools that will help you respond to difficult situations—those moments when you'd normally yell—in a more skillful way. You'll be learning specific communication skills in part II of this book, but for now, you can work on yelling less by planning out and precommitting to your new response.

Exercise: Create Your Yell-Less Plan

Plan out your ideal response to a difficult situation with your child. Precommitting to your choices will substantially increase your chances of success when you are angry. Choose a set of responses from the list below, then write out your plan in your *Raising Good Humans* journal, or post it in a handy location.

- **Tell yourself that you are safe:** "This is not an emergency. I can handle this."

- **Adopt a mantra to keep your perspective.** Repeat it to yourself several times when you feel as if you're about to explode: "He's only one. He's only one...," or "I don't have to 'win' here, I can let her save face," or "Choose love."

- **Create a mantra for yourself.** Remind yourself that you can make a choice to remain calm. Some mantras that help are:

"I am a ninja mom."

"When the kids start yelling, I get calmer."

"Still water."

"I choose peace."

"Relax, release, smile."

"This will pass. Breathe."

"Just be kind."

"It is what it is."

- **Take a break.** If you know you're going to lose it and you're on your very last nerve, put your baby or toddler in a safe spot, such as the playpen or crib, and walk away for a few minutes.

- **Five-Eight Breathing.** Breathe in for a count of five. Breathe out for a count of eight. (See previous exercise.)

- **Sigh it out.** This promotes relaxation. Repeat at least five or six times.

- **"Calm, Peace, Smile, Release."** Use this rhyme to help you breathe mindfully. As you breathe in, think "calm." As you breathe out, invite in "peace." As you breathe in, think "smile." As you breath out think "Release."

- **Mindful walking.** Walk slowly and deliberately. Breathe and let go of your anger and frustration. Place one foot down as you breathe in, place the other foot down and breathe out. Walk mindfully to release the tension in your body.

- **Think like a teacher.** Don't take misbehavior personally. Instead, look at it as a learning opportunity. Ask yourself: *What does my child need to learn and how can I teach him that?*

- **Whisper instead.** It's almost impossible to sound angry when you whisper. And it might help you find your sense of humor about the situation.

- **Use a funny voice or act out a character.** Channel your energy into being a robot!

- **Tense and release your muscles.** This will help calm yourself down.

- **Drop into child's pose.** (See "Strike a Pose" earlier in this chapter.)

- **Wait ten minutes—or twenty-four hours.** It's fine to wait ten minutes, or even until the next day, to come back and talk with your child about inappropriate language or behavior.

- **Ask for help from another adult.** Tag out of the situation so that you can calm down.

These tools may feel awkward at first if they are unfamiliar. Give yourself permission to "fake it till you make it," because as you practice, you'll be carving out new neural pathways in the brain. *Remember, what you practice grows stronger!*

Pick three or four of the above tools to practice regularly to form a new habit of response. Don't worry if you don't remember your new plan right away. What we're trying to do is move that moment of awareness earlier in the timeline. Initially, you're likely to remember this new plan *after* you've yelled. That's perfectly normal. Just keep trying. Put up reminders around the house (I'm a huge fan of sticky notes). As long as you keep trying, keep reminding yourself, and keep setting the intention to not yell—eventually you'll remember mid-yell, and then before you yell.

When we can start to take care of the energy of anger and let it pass through, we can be more present for our children and their big feelings. If we are able to stay grounded and stay with them during an upset, we demonstrate that there's nothing "wrong" with having big feelings, that it's simply a part of being human.

Check out this amazing win in this department that my Mindful Parenting student Valerie shared:

Valerie's Story

I had an aha moment today as my three-year-old went into a meltdown. He was trying to destroy things and throwing anything he could find. I had to go into my practiced mode of "I can't let you hurt, I can't let you destroy that" while remaining calm, blocking, and making sure he was physically safe. I used the mantra "I am helping you," and yet, after five minutes I could feel my anger rising.

I checked in and noticed the old pattern (which I have been aware of) of not accepting his big feelings and judging the behavior. I was thinking of it as something he is doing to me. I was able to reestablish my calm.

The tantrum continued, and a few minutes later I could feel the anger rise again. I checked in again, and this time I realized I was thinking, Why is he like this right now? What did I do/not do? What could I be doing better? Ugh, I must be doing something wrong...

It dawned on me in that moment that there was nothing to figure out, there was nothing to do other than be in this moment with him full-heartedly, not judging him for his tantrum, but showing him love. He may not have eaten enough for lunch and been over-hungry... which I realized was not my fault! It just was what it was. He was just getting out his frustration in a big way.

Constantly questioning and judging myself just leads to me being reactive in the moment rather than present. I can just accept his emotions for what they are without making such a big deal out of it (I am learning to let go of thoughts that "something is wrong with me"). In those moments, I have to breathe and remind myself I have no other place to be, nothing else to do except focus my attention on accepting him just as he is, and keeping him safe, and holding the boundary of not letting him destroy things in his frustration.

Whew! I made it through, and we were able to cuddle on the couch after it passed.

Taming your temper will help your relationship with your child grow stronger. As you practice these tools, you'll be giving your child something that most of us never had—a model of how to take care of the energy of anger. If you are able to stay present with your child's big feelings, rather than shame her emotions, she'll develop a healthy emotional intelligence— knowing that it's okay for her to have *all* emotions. You'll change the dynamic in your home, creating more peace and ease over time.

Disarming Your Triggers and Becoming More Present

Most of us weren't taught what to do when situations trigger anger inside, so when this inevitably happens, we're at a loss. Mostly we respond in the ways that our parents might have: yelling and losing it. Learning how to take care of our anger is a powerful practice. As we learn how to do this for ourselves, it's a two-for-one deal: we model compassionate and effective emotional management for our children too.

We can approach our anger from many different angles. We want to make sense of our childhood and start to understand where some of the triggers may be coming from. We need to make sure we don't have too much overall stress, which causes us to yell at our children. We can use tools to calm the body and the mind. We can look at our unique situation and create a personal plan to respond to our triggers in a healthier way. Finally, we can practice tools to acknowledge the feelings that arise—in ourselves and in our children—before they escalate to anger and rage.

Triggers can be deeply ingrained in our person. It usually takes some conscious effort to shift over to a more mindful response. Don't get discouraged when this doesn't happen overnight! It's bit-by-bit, over-time healing. In the next chapter, we're going to talk about the mental attitude we need to be able to sustain these practices during the time it takes to change. In the meantime, I leave you with these practices.

What to Practice this Week

- Sitting Meditation for five to ten minutes, four to six days per week

- Track Your Triggers

- Breathing Practices to Release Tension (Three-Part Breathing and Five-Eight Breathing)

- Your Yell-Less Plan

CHAPTER 3

Practicing Compassion—
It Begins with You

"Feeling compassion for ourselves in no way releases us from responsibility for our actions. Rather, it releases us from the self-hatred that prevents us from responding to our life with clarity and balance."

—Tara Brach

It was a clear fall day and time for my two-year-old's nap. I crossed my fingers for an easy nap time because I had work to finish. Unfortunately, no such luck. She whined relentlessly. She came downstairs and I took her back up—again and again. She was clearly exhausted and needed a nap. *I* needed this nap time. My temper rose. Upstairs, she started to throw things and come out of her room. I went upstairs again, shaking with frustration and feeling help-less. I grabbed her arms to put her on the bed—but I was too rough. Her fear was obvious. I felt her little arms beneath my strong hands and I realized, *This is how parents hurt their children. Oh. My. God.* Letting go, I left the room in tears.

As my tears flowed, my critical mind stepped in: *What's wrong with me? How could I do that? I'm a horrible mother* and on and on. My thoughts were harsh and bitter; I was saying things to myself that I would *never* say to another person. Did it help? No. It left me feeling weak, isolated, and incapable.

Our Inner Voice Matters

How we talk to ourselves after our mistakes can shape whether we shrink or grow from the experience. What we say to ourselves in the privacy of our own thoughts really *matters*. Why? To borrow a metaphor from best-selling self-help author and motivational speaker Wayne Dyer: If I have an orange, what will come out when I squeeze it? Juice, of course. But what kind of juice will come out? Not pomegranate or kiwi. Orange juice. And like that orange, when we are squeezed, *what's inside is what will come out.*

What comes out of *you* when you are squeezed? That inner evil step-mother? If your inner voice is harsh and critical, then that's what's likely to come out with your child too. For me, in that moment when I was really squeezed, harshness came out. Negative, disparaging criticism came out. Because that's what was inside. And it left me feeling completely incapacitated.

Holly's Story

Holly was a working mom living alone with her three boys. Her eight-year-old son was having nightmares, which kept them both up at night, and his exhaustion came out as anger during the day. One morning, she was showering after yet another sleepless night when he walked in, enraged about something. He pulled on the shower curtain and the rod gave way, exposing Holly. She lost it, yelling and slapping his face.

Afterward, she felt overwhelmed by shame, guilt, and regret for days. She couldn't stop crying, paralyzed by her inner voice. Holly told me, "I didn't want to eat and I couldn't sleep. I kept thinking I was a terrible, terrible mother. I didn't deserve to have my children."

After a week, her mother came to visit and was appalled at her daughter's state. Holly said, "I was useless. I wasn't helping anyone. The self-shaming wasn't helping me to reconnect with my children." Her harsh, judgmental inner voice filled her with shame and made a bad situation worse.

Holly is far from alone. Way too many of us respond to our mistakes and shortcomings by mercilessly judging and criticizing ourselves. Our inner voice can flood us with shaming thoughts that don't help. Negative self-talk and self-shaming don't make us more effective or more peaceful parents. In fact, *it does the reverse.* Shame leaves us feeling trapped, powerless, and isolated. When we feel like that, we're not able to bring a kind and compassionate presence to our children.

Shame Doesn't Help

Researcher Brené Brown has helped us understand the difference between guilt and shame. *Shame* is a feeling of badness about the self. *Guilt* is about behavior—a feeling of "conscience" from having done something wrong or against our values. Her research has shown that guilt can be helpful and adaptive, while shame is destructive and doesn't help us change our behavior. As Brown (2012) puts it:

> *"Shame corrodes the very part of us that believes we are capable of change."*

When you feel like a terrible person, it's almost impossible to empower yourself to make a change.

Furthermore, if we want our children to have self-compassion, we must *model* it. For example, if you have the habit of self-shaming, your child will pick that up. As I've said before, our kids may not be so great at doing what we say, but they are great at doing what we do. This is how harmful generational patterns are passed down. That harsh critical voice from a parent becomes the inner voice of the child. Then that child becomes a parent and the habit of harshness comes out again.

Don't Shoot the Second Arrow

You can think of self-shaming as the "second arrow." In a Buddhist parable, the Buddha once asked a student, "If a person is struck by an arrow, is it painful? If the person is struck by a second arrow, is it even more painful?"

He then went on to explain, "In life, we can't always control the first arrow," meaning that difficult and painful things will happen in everyone's life. However, "The second arrow is our reaction to the first. The second arrow *is optional*."

Our harsh criticism is the mind's second arrow. It does not help us heal from the first arrow wound. In fact, the second arrow of shaming and blaming others and ourselves is optional. We have a choice. We can choose to bring kindness and self-compassion to our suffering instead.

The Self-Compassion Cure

Imagine if, instead of self-shaming, we could offer ourselves the kindness and understanding of a good friend. How might that change things? Research is showing that this approach helps us grow and learn from our own mistakes better than the old paradigm of condemnation.

Kristin Neff, researcher, author, and professor at the University of Texas at Austin, has dedicated her life's work to the study of compassion and self-compassion. Neff (2011a) writes:

> *These are not just "nice" ideas. There is an ever-increasing body of research that attests to the motivational power of self-compassion. Self-compassionate people set high standards for themselves, but they aren't as upset when they don't meet their goals. Instead, research shows that they're more likely to set new goals for themselves after failure rather than wallowing in feelings of frustration and disappointment. Self-compassionate people are more likely to take responsibility for their past mistakes, while acknowledging them with greater emotional equanimity. Research also shows that self-compassion helps people engage in health-ier behaviors like sticking to their weight-loss goals, exercising, quitting smoking, and seeking medical care when needed.*

How to Talk to Yourself

Neff breaks down self-compassion into three elements: *self-kindness*, *common humanity*, and *mindfulness*. So how do we begin to practice self-compassion instead of self-judgment? We can start by noticing and interrupting our negative self-talk. Your regular meditation practice will help you do this by giving you more clarity and awareness of your thoughts in general. It doesn't matter how often you notice that disparaging, critical voice, just try to catch it in mindful awareness. As soon as you catch it, you might say to yourself, "Hello, old pattern." Doing this, you interrupt the old, unhealthy habit. This pattern of negative self-talk may have been something you've unconsciously "practiced" for years, so it's likely to be quite strong and tenacious. It's not likely that you'll ever get rid of the critical mind, but you *can* create a new pattern. That's the gift of *neuroplasticity* (discussed in chapter 1): what you practice grows stronger.

Self-Kindness

What would you say to your best friend in a moment like Holly's shower incident? Probably something like, "You're *not* a terrible mom. You felt threatened and you reacted. You're a good person."

That's exactly how I want you to practice changing your internal dialogue. Instead of indulging in the harsh inner critic, find truthful, kind words that soothe your frayed nervous system. Think *helping* instead of *shaming*. Talk to yourself as you would to your best friend. It may feel unfamiliar and awkward initially, but with repetition your new habit of kindness will get stronger.

The last time I yelled at my daughter, I regretted it immediately. I apologized and hugged her when we were both ready. Instead of the harsh inner critic, I practiced self-compassion: I acknowledged my critical thoughts: "I'm *having a thought that* I'm a bad mother." Then I offered myself as much sympathy and kindness as I could muster. I tried to remember how difficult parenting is and how hard it is to tame my temper sometimes. With that kind of nourishing internal response, instead of feeling paralyzed by shame, I was able to move my attention back to taking care of my daughter—a win for both of us!

Common Humanity

The second element of self-compassion is recognizing that *we are not the only ones who make mistakes*. Neff calls this "common humanity vs. isolation."

We have thoughts like, *I shouldn't have yelled at my daughter. Good parents never yell the way I did.*

When we think like that, we feel alone in our suffering, whereas the truth is that we are *all* mistake-making humans and imperfect parents. Our imperfections are what make us human. There are certainly moments when I—a Mindful Mama Mentor—have made mistakes with my children that I regret. It's time to recognize that none of us is alone in this.

Mindfulness

Finally, in order to be compassionate with ourselves we have to *recognize*, through mindfulness, that we are suffering. We must practice noticing the thoughts that arise and remain objective about them. We need to work on attention to how we treat ourselves when mistakes happen, and we must practice offering ourselves sympathy and kindness.

Think of all the suffering you inflict upon yourself—through harsh self-criticism and self-judgment. Once you notice these thoughts, you can choose another way—offering yourself compassion and kindness when you don't meet your standards. Mindfulness helps you to not get caught up in and swept away by your negative reactions.

Practice Loving-Kindness

One life-changing way to build your compassion muscle is through the ancient practice of *loving-kindness*, either through formal meditation or compassionate thoughts you pepper throughout your day. The term "loving-kindness" is a translation of the Pali word "*metta*," which means "friendly, amicable, benevolent, affectionate, kind, or sympathetic love." It's the perfect antidote to that mean voice inside.

How do you practice? Essentially, you start by simply generating the feeling of loving-kindness toward someone who's easy to love. Then you practice extending it to yourself, then to those with whom you have difficulties.

As with mindfulness, simply reading about loving-kindness will not give you the skills! This is a *practice* that, when done regularly, can change your interior landscape, turning down the volume on that harsh inner voice and providing a loving alternative. Don't think you can only practice during difficult moments! Just like building muscle at the gym, you build your self-compassion muscle bit by bit over time.

Practice: Loving-Kindness

Loving-kindness is a form of love that is active. It's a way to look at ourselves and others with kindness instead of reflexive criticism. You can use this written-out form or listen to the audio recording available at http://www.raising-goodhumansbook.com. Then build this practice into your meditation routine.

Sit in an alert and comfortable position. Let your mind be spacious and your heart be kind and soft. Let your body relax.

Feel your breath travel in and out of your body. Notice any thoughts that pop up, then refocus your attention on your breath.

Notice any emotions that are present. Let your body soften a bit as you exhale.

Picture someone in your life who has truly cared for you, someone who is easy to love. Picture this person in your mind and recite the following phrases:

May you be safe

May you be happy

May you be healthy

May you live with ease

You are welcome to adjust the words. Repeat the phrases over and over, letting the feelings come fully into your body and mind.

Now practice loving-kindness toward yourself. You can picture yourself as you are now or picture yourself as a four-year-old child. Say to yourself the following phrases (or a variation that resonates with you). As you repeat these phrases, you can picture yourself suffused by the light of loving-kindness:

May I be safe

May I be happy

May I be healthy

May I live with ease

At times, it may feel rote or awkward, or even bring up irritation. If this happens, it is especially important to be patient and kind toward yourself. Accept what arises with a spirit of friendliness.

Once you feel you have established some sense of loving-kindness, expand your meditation to include others: friends, community members, all beings on earth.

You may even include the difficult people in your life, wishing that they too be filled with loving-kindness and peace.

As you make loving-kindness a part of your life, you'll gain more peace, ease, and kindness, and you'll naturally give that to others more frequently. Self-help guru Wayne Dyer taught this message throughout his life, saying, "If love and joy are what you want to give and receive, change your life by changing what's inside."

Similarly, shame researcher Brené Brown wrote in *Daring Greatly* (2012, p. 177), "We can't give people what we don't have. Who we are matters immeasurably more than what we know or who we want to be." Parenting is guaranteed to squeeze you—to bring up all of your unresolved issues. So it is a beautiful opportunity to be intentional about what you want in your life. What you practice grows stronger.

Modeling Kindness and Empathy

When my youngest daughter was two years old, she would run over to where her older sister was playing, grab her toy, and jumble up the whole game—all to get her sister's attention. Kids are often complete disasters when it comes to relating. They are, *by definition*, immature (human brains are not fully developed until we're in our twenties). They need guidance and modeling from us on how to get along in the world.

Happily, kids naturally care about others. Just as we realize that *what we practice grows stronger* for ourselves, it bears remembering that what we practice grows within our children as well. We can model what we want to see: kindness and empathy. Think of kindness as the *quality* of being friendly, generous, and considerate—wanting to see others happy—and empathy as the *way* we do so.

Give and Receive Kindness

Why kindness? Shouldn't we be talking about respect and authority when it comes to parenting? Though we all want our children to be kind to themselves and others—and we know that kindness helps us all get along in the world and live a happy life—sometimes as parents we think that we have to use force, manipulation, and fear to get our kids to do what we want. That is, to get them to respect our authority. However, force and manipulation are not the same as authority, and fear is not the same as respect. We forget that if we use force, manipulation, and fear with our children, they will learn to use these tactics with others. Instead, if we want them to value kindness, we must *practice* kindness—even while we hold limits. Plus, kindness and empathy drive connection, and connection drives cooperation.

Kindness begins with ourselves, so working to interrupt and replace our harsh inner critic is a great start. We can look at our other attitudes and beliefs as well. For example, do you think taking care of yourself is selfish? Many of us were taught that idea or at least internalized it somewhere along our journey. We may have learned that in order to be a good person, we need to be "selfless," taking care of others, even at the expense of personal well-being. However, kindness toward ourselves is an essential foundation of good relationships with others. It's not selfish—it's wise.

Remember that orange metaphor: "When you are squeezed, what comes out?" If we practice being friendly, generous, and considerate with ourselves, then we can be friendly, generous, and considerate with our children, who will then learn to be friendly, generous, and considerate in turn. Beautiful cycle, right?

Empathy, the Parenting Superpower

As I put it above, empathy is the *way* we do kindness. At its simplest, empathy is our awareness of the feelings and emotions of other people. It's the link between self and others, how we understand what others are experiencing. Instead of having the "Oh, poor you" attitude toward someone who's suffering, it's "Wow, that sucks, I know what that feels like."

Empathy is essential for creating stronger bonds with our children. It is also a capacity that can be learned and nurtured. How? By practicing tuning in to an other's emotional cues and taking the other's perspective.

Theresa Wiseman (1996), a nursing scholar in the United Kingdom, has studied empathy, and this is how she breaks it down:

- **To be able to see the world as others see it.** This requires putting our own stuff aside to see the situation through our loved ones' eyes.

- **To be nonjudgmental.** Judgment of other people's situations discounts their experience and is an attempt to protect ourselves from the pain of the situation.

- **To understand another person's feelings.** We have to be in touch with our own feelings in order to understand someone else's. Again, this requires putting our own stuff aside to focus on our loved ones.

- **To communicate our understanding of another person's feelings.** Rather than saying, "At least you..." or "It could be worse...," try: "I've been there, and that really hurts" or "It sounds like you are in a hard place now. Tell me more about it." This is an approach that may not come intuitively. But we'll go into more detail on speaking this way later in this book.

Keisha's Story

Keisha's daughter wanted her earrings changed out—a frustrating task filled with tears. Keisha dreaded these moments because her own anger would rise quickly, which only seemed to exacerbate her girl's crying. But one day Keisha took a pause and said, "Self, you are getting angry— why? Because I think she's not being 'brave' right now. She's crying. When I was growing up, I was taught to 'toughen up' and not to cry. But she is not me, and now is not then. It hurts, she's scared, and that's real."

Practicing empathy, Keisha paused to identify and see beyond her own stuff, so that she could be present to what was really happening for

*her daughter. She was able to hug her daughter and say, "I see
you're scared and I understand. I'm sorry this is uncomfortable.
Let's take a deep breath together, and when you're ready we can do
the other earring."*

Empathy is our parenting superpower—it's the skill that will help our children achieve the holy grail of their own emotional regulation. When we can sense what our children are feeling and experiencing—and be present with them—we are building connection and attunement.

In *Parenting from the Inside Out*, Daniel Siegel and Mary Hartzell (2014, p. 63) say that empathy allows a child to "feel felt, to feel that she exists within the mind of the parent." When we parent with empathy, we become more connected to our children and can understand where they are coming from. It helps resolve every conflict more easily.

Note that offering empathy requires that our own cup is full. Making self-care a priority is vital to being able to offer kindness and empathy. Remember, self-care is not a "nice to have" kind of thing. It's your *right* and your *responsibility*.

And don't worry: even if you've fallen short on empathy recently, you can always cultivate it. As social creatures, we are "wired" to be empathetic, yet it is also something we can learn and practice.

Chill Out the Judging Mind

We all have a critical voice in our heads that continually passes judgment on ourselves and others. Remember how those harsh self-judgments can leave us unable to grow and learn? Harsh judgments have a similar effect on our kids, sapping their self-confidence. Judgments and criticism wound our children, sending them the message: "I don't like and accept you as you are."

Yet our minds are constantly judging! When we feel uncomfortable or see a behavior in our children that makes us cringe inside, judgmental thoughts naturally arise. That's completely normal. Your mindfulness practice will help you to notice these thoughts and interrupt them. As soon as you label a thought as "judging," you've already lessened its power.

Try to keep in mind that children who *act* bad *feel* bad—this can help to bring out our natural (if slightly buried at times) compassion. Too often we don't take our children's suffering seriously. The itchy tag doesn't seem like a big deal to us, so why make such a fuss? Who cares if one child called the other one short?

But when we dismiss our children's problems, our little ones feel overlooked and uncared for. Instead, we can use mindfulness to notice our thoughts, then consciously *choose* to respond with kindness and empathy to our children's behavior. When we do, we strengthen our connection to our children, making it more likely that they'll respond cooperatively in the future.

Your judgmental voice can also turn on your mindfulness practice. It might say, "I can't do this" or "I'll never be able to do this" or "Other people are much better at this." Regardless of whether we are judging our parenting, our practice, or our kids, it helps to stop and recognize the judging mind when it arises. Test this out. Try out consciously cultivating an attitude of acceptance and friendly curiosity, and see how it feels and how it affects your relationships.

Empathy, kindness, and nonjudgment are hugely beneficial attitudes for us as parents… and they are hard to remember when we're in a hurry and hurrying along our kids. That's why, as we round out this chapter on cultivating kindness from the inside out, it's imperative that we talk a little bit about *patience*.

Patience? Are You Kidding Me?

Do you remember your mom telling you to "be patient" as a child? I do. It was never my strong suit, and even the word can leave an unpleasant taste in my mouth (hello, childhood baggage!). Yet, parents in this incredibly fast-paced world need patience desperately. Our nervous system receives the simple act of *hurrying* as a threat, which triggers the stress response.

When we practice patience, we are less reactive. We can slow down to allow time for shoes to go on, remembering that it's not the end of the world if we're five minutes late. We can take that essential moment of pause to be more fully aware of the feelings and motivations involved in any given parenting moment. It really only takes the space of a few breaths. This gives us time to realize what is *really* happening in the present moment.

I struggle with impatience daily. My "habit-energy" is to get things done efficiently so that I can move on to the next moment. This lack of patience is usually the culprit when I have stressful conflicts with my children. I want to leave the house *right now*. When my impatience gets the better of me, I am a reactionary and grumpy mom. If I can summon some patience, things generally go much more smoothly.

A few years ago, I walked into the living room where my daughters were playing with a friend. They'd overturned chairs, draped the dining room furniture with scarves, and covered nearly every surface with stuffed animals and blocks. I wanted the whole thing cleaned up *now*. The situation called for patience, not my strongest suit. But, learning from explosive moments in the past, I took the time to talk to my daughters calmly. Apparently, their stuffed elephant needed a bandage in order to recover from an injury. Armed with this understanding, I was able to wait for bandage application before I shared my own need for the space to be tidied. The bonus of slowing down was that it gave me time to speak more skillfully, rather than bark out orders. Patience let me see my daughters' needs in that moment, and our day was not disrupted by fighting and yelling.

Can we allow things to unfold at their own speed, rather than trying to control the situation? As you know, a child's speed is much slower than an adult's. Children are naturally in-the-moment creatures and curious about the world around them. Too often, we adults are indoctrinating them into the hurry-all-the-time habit. Instead, we can practice allowing more space and time for children to move at their own pace, rather than always rushing them.

This isn't easy—trust me, I'm right there with you. That's why we call it a *practice*. We're not going to be perfectly patient all the time, and that's okay. However, the more we rush, the more likely it is that our lifestyle induces stress and anxiety in our kids. Slowing down pays off.

The patience mindset comes with a caveat. It's easy to be patient when things are going well. But, in fact, patience is particularly helpful to nurture when your mind is agitated and your thoughts are running wild: to strengthen it, you need to practice it in lots of situations. I urge you to practice being patient with *yourself*. This parenting thing isn't easy! It's totally normal to feel like an enraged rhino at times. Expect unskillful moments and practice patience in regard to your own progress in building patience!

Practice: Mantras for Patience

Pick one or two of these mantras, write them on sticky notes, and post them strategically around your home. Repeat to yourself as needed!

I help my child most when I am calm.

When the kids start yelling, I get calmer.

I choose peace.

[Breathing in] I am love. *[Breathing out]* I can pause.

Relax, release, smile.

This will pass. Breathe.

Just be kind.

It is what it is.

Patience with your meditation practice. Patience is an important factor in your mindfulness meditation too. Cultivate patience by intentionally reminding yourself that there is nowhere to go and nothing else to do when you find the mind judging, agitated, or fidgety. Give yourself room to have these experiences. Why? Because you're having them! When things come up in meditation, they are your current reality. That's how life is unfolding in this moment.

Patience in your life. Remember that we don't have to fill up every moment with entertainment, distractions, and activity. Life gets better when we make space and time to absorb each moment rather than rushing to the next thing. When we allow some spacious, unstructured time around activities, we enjoy them as a family even more. Downtime is a good thing.

Stop Trying So Hard

"Okay, Hunter," you may be saying to yourself, "Now I have a big list of to-dos, including practicing loving-kindness, noticing my unhelpful thoughts, practicing patience, and letting go of judgment. I'm going to start getting to work right now!"

On the contrary, I invite you to chill out a little bit and allow these ideas to sink in (come back and reread this chapter as needed in the future). Why?

Chances are, you've been trained from childhood toward achievement and goal setting. When we are so accustomed to striving like this, it becomes hard to simply rest in the present moment with whatever is going on. We tend to say to ourselves, "If only I were… [more calm, more intelligent, a harder worker, in better health, wealthier], then I would be okay. But right now, I am not okay." The feeling of *not* being okay drives us on to improve, right *now*! This sets us running on a hamster wheel of insecurity—and, as with all hamster wheels, we run and run and get nowhere. Instead, I'm going to ask you to cultivate the attitude of *nonstriving*.

Jon Kabat-Zinn (2013) points out that striving can be a real obstacle in meditation—because in meditation, there's no other goal than to simply be yourself as you are right now. When we can be fully in the present moment and accept ourselves exactly as we are now, then we've gone a long way toward reducing the stress and anxiety that makes us reactive in the first place. So I invite you to be disciplined about your practices… and relax.

Letting go of striving (which is always directed at some future state) helps us become more present to what is actually happening. It doesn't mean not making an effort or not applying ourselves in practice, parenting, or life. Instead, it means showing up, applying ourselves, and letting go of the outcome. It is truly healing and restorative for us to let go of our agendas from time to time and simply let life unfold. Our children also thrive when, instead of constantly shuttling them from place to place, we give them space to just be.

Nonstriving does not mean inaction; instead it means holding things lightly. We all have goals and aspirations, but can we soften our grip on them? To take a commonplace example: you may have the aspiration for your child to go to college—a wonderful, beneficial goal. But if you push too hard, your striving can create debilitating anxiety for him. The mindset of non-striving asks us to hold that aspiration lightly, knowing that things are already okay as they are, and that whatever unfolds will be something we can handle.

Go for Good Enough

In parenting, nonstriving leads us to the idea of "good-enough parenting." The good-enough parent is a concept derived from the work of pediatrician and psychoanalyst D. W. Winnicott (1973). The basic idea is to chill out a little bit, because along the way things are going to go wrong, and your child is going to struggle here and there, but these struggles aren't the end of the world. In fact, they *help* your child develop resilience.

Good-enough parenting tells us that we don't need to strive to be perfect parents, and we should not expect perfection from our children. Problems will occur in every family, and reacting with blame, shame, and harsh criticism does not help. Instead, can we remember that imperfections in all human beings are unavoidable—especially for kids? Can we expect our children to make mistakes? Can we let go of our own striving for perfection?

In fact, when we allow ourselves to be human, and model healing in our relationships, we model that for our kids. They *need* to see you mess up, make amends, and still value yourself—so they know how to do it themselves.

Kindness from the Inside Out

Cultivating loving-kindness and awareness of your inner voice can have a deep and lasting impact on your relationship with your child. You are half of the parent-child relationship. It's time to take responsibility for what you are bringing to the table. When you start to transform your thoughts from harsh criticism and judgment to empathy and acceptance of your humanity, this translates into more empathy and acceptance of others. Who you are as a person inside counts quite a lot in terms of who you want your child to be.

As you continue to develop your sitting meditation practice, these other practices will become easier. Cultivating more awareness of what's really happening in the present moment (rather than hanging onto our stories or thoughts), is the foundation for all meaningful change—because if you can't see it, you can't make a different choice. Increasing your awareness of the inner critical voice may feel uncomfortable and discouraging initially, but I encourage you to not give up. We all have negativity bias to contend with. The fact that you are aware of it will help you to *not* act from it.

Remember, *reading about this is not what makes the change.* It's all about practice. Loving-kindness might feel silly and awkward at first, but I assure you it's a powerful practice that has lasting and meaningful benefits. Changing the inner voice to a kind one may be the crucial inner shift that allows you to communicate more skillfully using the strategies in part II of this book.

Our next chapter is the final one on the inner work of living what we want our children to learn. You'll soon learn how to mindfully take care of difficult feelings.

What to Practice This Week

- Sitting Meditation or body scan meditation for five to ten minutes, four to six days per week
- Loving-Kindness Practice four to six days per week
- Noticing the judging mind
- Practicing kindness, empathy, and self-compassion
- Mantras for Patience

CHAPTER 4

Taking Care of Difficult Feelings

"The impulse to eschew the unpleasant leads to avoidance; avoidance leads to aversion; aversion leads to fear; fear leads to hatred; hatred leads to aggression. Unwittingly, the oh-so-natural instinct to avoid the unpleasant becomes the root of hatred. It leads to war: war within, war without."

—Stephen Cope

A child crying or having a tantrum can bring about a special kind of pain for us parents. When my oldest daughter was two years old, she would do what toddlers do when they are at the end of their limited resources—lose it. And I would start to feel like I wanted to crawl out of my skin. It felt *unbearable*. So I would lose it too. From too many experiences, I can assure you that the mommy tantrum is *not* an effective parenting tool. It left us both feeling sad and chaotic. It was the kind of emotional messiness that many of us don't anticipate when becoming parents.

In previous chapters, we've explored some of the reasons why these big reactions are triggered in us and how mindfulness and self-compassion can heal these old hurts. Now we're going to look at resources you can use on a day-to-day basis to take care of difficult feelings for yourself—and, then, for your child.

Habitual Responses to Feelings

We often spend a lot of energy trying to push our feelings under the surface so we don't feel them, and we model the same to our kids. We seem to forget that we *all* have feelings—of *all* kinds—good, bad, and ugly. Suppressing our feelings is another unhealthy emotional pattern that previous generations have passed down to us. The story we've been told is: "Don't have those feelings. They make me uncomfortable. You are wrong for having those feelings." So we try to push them under, forgetting that they will pop up later with more force than ever—usually at the least convenient time.

Many of us respond to pain or discomfort in one of two ways: we either attempt to block out our feelings or we become flooded by the emotions we've been trying to suppress.

Blocking: We may try to stop or deny the discomfort by denying our feelings, distracting ourselves, or self-medicating with food, alcohol, or drugs. These moves are ultimately ineffective and unhealthy. This is because the uncomfortable feeling actually has a function: it is often a sign that some corrective action needs to take place. Missing the sign can result in some harm to ourselves or others. And, of course, self-medicating creates a whole host of problems for our emotional and physical health, including addiction.

Becoming flooded: This happens when we become overwhelmed by our feelings or lost in our thoughts, especially when we're drowning in our fears and judgments ("I can't stand this!" "How could they/I have been so stupid?!" and so on). Becoming flooded by fears and sadness can lead to a sense of hopelessness and powerlessness. Becoming flooded by anger—exploding and yelling—pushes others away, leading to more bad feelings. Things get worse, never better.

Exercise: What Are Your Habitual Responses to Feelings?

When we have uncomfortable feelings, our habitual responses may range from grabbing a tub of gummy worms to raging at our kids. What are your habitual responses? Below are some common ways that people deal with their feelings. In your *Raising Good Humans* journal, write down the responses that you notice in yourself:

Blocking	Becoming Flooded
Distractions: screen time, social media	Overwhelm
Food, shopping, alcohol, drugs	Yelling, aggression
Shame	Powerlessness
Guilt	Hopelessness

When you've identified your common responses, start to notice them in everyday life. Get curious, like a scientist. Then, select a time to practice staying nonreactive instead. Mindfully notice the feelings and sensations that arise. Notice that it's possible to breathe and sit through those feelings. Journal on your experience.

Blocking and becoming flooded are two sides of the same coin. They are the extremes we swing between rather than walking the middle path of mindfully *feeling* and processing our emotions as they arise. If you experience blocking and flooding, it's likely that some form of this unhealthy habitual pattern was modeled in your family. Sans effort on your part, you are likely to pass down this pattern to your child. What's a mindful parent to do? Let's look at that middle path of healthy emotional expression.

The Middle Path: Mindful Acceptance

In the middle path, you are neither pushing away difficult feelings or situations, nor are you subsumed by them. Instead, you learn to accept and *feel* the sensations brought about by your emotions, which allows them to pass in due course.

Resistance Makes It Hurt More

When we're upset, we obviously don't want to feel that way, so blocking or fighting those feelings is our instinctive response. We want to avoid uncomfortable things. The problem is that we can't avoid all of life's hurts, and our resistance to them when they arise makes things worse. This is such a common human behavior that Buddhists came up with an equation for it:

Pain x Resistance = Suffering

Fighting against the reality of our pain makes it worse—it creates suffering. The equation also says that it's possible to experience pain without suffering—they are not the same thing.

Let's say you feel frustrated and angry at your child. Then you feel bad about yourself for having that anger at all. You try to block your feelings, triggering an eventual explosion, or you allow them to flood you, taking up way more time and space than they need to. Your resistance has *added an additional layer of suffering*. The suffering makes it harder to see clearly in the moment and harder to respond thoughtfully. And the extra layers of judgment make it more likely that your conflict will continue to simmer under the surface. It is the second arrow we talked about in chapter 3.

Acceptance Makes It Hurt Less

Psychologist Carl Jung long ago said that "what you resist not only persists, but will grow in size." Today we abbreviate this to "What you resist persists," pointing to the ineffectiveness of blocking out our feelings (Seltzer 2016). Avoidance leads to suffering and keeps us from living fully. I like to think of our feelings as toddlers: they will not give us any peace until we truly *see* and *hear* them. That means acknowledging and accepting our uncomfortable emotions.

Accepting the reality of your painful feelings will put you on a faster track to healing that pain. As counterintuitive as it may seem, accepting and staying with that uncomfortable "I've got to get out of here" feeling often lessens the discomfort and sometimes allows it to completely disappear. Think about it as going to your edges and then softening. If you have ever practiced yoga, you may have experienced this—in yoga you go to the edge of your discomfort and rest there. And you find that the discomfort shifts.

"Acceptance," however, is a fraught word. To be clear: acceptance does not mean that you *like* the emotion that you are experiencing. It just means that you acknowledge that this is a part of your experience in this moment.

You are accepting the reality of what is. It also does not mean that you are passive and don't take action to change situations. Acceptance does not mean that you say yes to all outside people and circumstances. And it does not mean that you say yes to limiting beliefs. Continue to interrupt and change harmful thoughts like, "I'm no good at this" or "I'm a bad parent"—fight the good fight there. However, you can still accept the uncomfortable emotions that arise. They are there—deal with them squarely—because what you resist persists.

Acknowledgment Boosts Acceptance

A simple way to practice accepting our feelings is the acknowledgment practice from chapter 1. When an uncomfortable feeling arises, rather than pushing through to the next thing on your to-do list, blocking your feelings with distraction, or losing it, you can internally *say what you feel*. This simple labeling can provide a lot of relief. I find that if I acknowledge my anxiety, for instance, by pausing and saying to myself, "Hello, anxiety, I see you there," it gives me a moment to stop and feel what's happening in my body. Labeling loosens anxiety's hold on me, giving me the breathing space I need to let it pass.

A note about acceptance: when you practice accepting the emotions that arise, don't do it *with the intention of changing it*. That's a subtle form of resistance that can keep things stuck. Just like our children, our emotions don't like to be manipulated. They want to be fully seen and heard.

Feel to Radically Heal

A robust acceptance—fully immersing ourselves in our senses—may just be the key to emotional freedom. French behavioral and communication expert Luc Nicon suggests that all of our mental efforts to tame our feelings may actually backfire (Bertelli 2018). His research suggests that when we *fully* immerse ourselves in the sensory input of our feelings—*without* deep breathing or other management techniques—they dissipate and dissolve most easily. He calls this method by its French acronym, TIPI (which translates to "technique to identify subconscious fears"). It's surprisingly simple to practice: the following exercise will guide you through it.

Practice: TIPI

To start regulating your emotional patterns, you need to fully feel the physical sensations that accompany those emotions. According to TIPI, it doesn't matter why the feeling has arisen. All that matters is that the feeling is there. Do not try to understand or control it. Do not blame.

Follow these simple steps whenever an emotion arises:

1. *Close your eyes.*

2. *Pay attention to two or three physical sensations in your body (stiffness or tightness in your throat or chest, etc.). Mentally label, or note, the sensations to keep your mind fully present.*

3. *Let those sensations evolve, continuing to note them. Allow breathing to become shallow, if that is the natural evolution of the sensation.*

4. *Observe with curiosity and without interfering or trying to understand or control. Simply notice the sensations until your body restores a state of calmness. (Yes, this is easier said than done).*

Open your eyes. This entire process may take less than a minute or several.

Practice TIPI daily, as emotions arise, over the course of a week or two to test this practice out for yourself. Like a scientist studying yourself, note the effects in your Raising Good Humans *journal.*

When I heard about TIPI, I was skeptical. So I tested it out myself, and much to my surprise, this very simple method is truly effective. I found that when I got my thoughts and stories out of the way and fully immersed myself in my body, my body's natural capacity to heal opened up. Our minds can get in the way of healing difficult feelings; our thoughts can resist the full acceptance and immersion that healing requires.

In her book *Radical Acceptance* (2003), Insight Meditation teacher Tara Brach shares another way for us to experience the power of acceptance. She invites us to practice saying yes to all of the feelings that arise. If our resistance is a mental no, then yes can be an effective antidote. Try this out for yourself:

Exercise: Experiencing Yes vs. No

Find a comfortable place to sit quietly. Bring to mind an emotion that you find yourself resisting. Make sure this emotion is nontraumatic. Pay attention to your throat, chest, and stomach. Notice how the emotion feels in your body.

Now start to say *no* to this feeling. Repeat the no for a minute or so. Note how the no feels in your body. Take a few deep breaths.

Now start to say *yes* to the feeling. Repeat the yes for a minute or so. Notice how the yes feels in your body.

Take notes comparing the two experiences in your *Raising Good Humans* journal.

When you try the "Experiencing Yes vs. No" exercise, you'll likely find that *no* increases the tension in the body, while *yes* softens you, giving you space to accept the feelings. Just as in childbirth, relaxing the body helps ease the pain. Relaxing your resistance will help ease the pain of your difficult feeling. Plus, as you do this work, you are modeling healthy emotional responses for your child. It's a two-for-one deal!

Being Mindful of the Roots of Our Resistance

Although these words about acceptance may strike an inner note of truth, it can still be very difficult to allow ourselves to feel uncomfortable feelings. For those of us who experienced some level of emotional abuse in our upbringing, those tough feelings of anger, anxiety, grief, embarrassment, remorse, sadness, and more can feel deeply *unacceptable*. Perhaps we were told: "Don't cry" or "Go to your room until you're in a better mood" or "I'll give you something to cry about" or "Don't be so *sensitive*." These harmful messages turn into a critical voice inside our heads, preventing us from doing the deeper work of healing.

The only way out of our difficult feelings is *through*. We *have* to feel our feelings in order to process them in a healthy way. If our emotions are not felt fully, they become bottled up and create all kinds of problems as that emotion leaks out in unhealthy ways. Therefore, I grant you permission to feel *all the feels*. Allow yourself to join the sister- and brotherhood of those who feel their emotions wholeheartedly—and thus do not allow their emotions to run them. Practicing accepting your emotions, whether by using TIPI or saying yes, is a great start.

Still, it can be hard to "feel all the feelings," and sometimes it's not appropriate! Most of us can practice mindfully and intentionally feeling our difficult and uncomfortable emotions so that they can be released in a healthy way. But how do we let ourselves feel when expressing our emotions wasn't always safe? Here are two useful guidelines:

- **Check your environment.** It's always wise to make sure that you are in a safe, calm, and stable place before you begin processing difficult feelings. Think about where you are. If you feel like you can close your eyes, then chances are good that it's an acceptable space.

- **Get some help.** Are the feelings that are arising traumatic and deeply triggering? That is, will thinking about certain events and feelings leave you feeling out of control or worse? If so, it's a good idea to seek out the support of a therapist to help you process these traumatic emotions. Finding the help you need to heal these intense and triggering old wounds will pave the way for mindful contact with a wider range of feelings, including the uncomfortable feelings that come up in your parenting.

RAIN: A Mindful Path Through Difficult Feelings

RAIN is an acronym that can help you remember the mindful way through difficult emotions:

Recognize

Allow or accept

Investigate

Nurture

How does it work? Let's find out.

Recognize

The mindful way through difficult emotions starts when we *recognize* that we're having an emotion and label it. Is it anxiety, fear, helplessness, overwhelm, sadness, grief, embarrassment, frustration, or something else? To recognize the emotion, name it in your head: "anxiety" (or whatever it is). As soon as you label it, you bring the verbal part of your brain in the prefrontal cortex back online. When we recognize, we take that vital step away from blocking our feelings. We acknowledge that this is the reality of the situation in this moment.

When you recognize your feeling, say to yourself, "I am *feeling* _____," rather than "I *am* _____." For example, "I am feeling frustrated" rather than "I am frustrated." This helps us to stop identifying ourselves with that feeling, providing a bit of breathing room. After all, we don't say, "I am a broken foot." We say, "I *have* a broken foot." Allow yourself that bit of objectivity with your emotions too.

Allow

After recognizing the feeling, the next step is more of a nonaction: *allow* it to be there. You can think of this as the practice of acceptance we talked about earlier. How do you do this? There are many ways. You can use the "Experiencing Yes vs. No" practice, if that resonates with you.

Another way is one I learned from Zen master Thich Nhat Hanh, who told us to imagine that we are holding our difficult feeling in our arms like a baby. We can then say to that feeling, "It's okay that you are here, dear _____ [name your emotion]. I'm here for you. I'm going to take care of you." This practice may feel silly initially, but I've found it to be a deep and profound way to get to a place of acceptance, especially with emotions triggered by my children.

Investigate

Next, we gently and mindfully *investigate* why this feeling has arisen. When you are not pushing your feeling away or wallowing in it, you can find the space to be *curious* about it. Try this: imagine that you are a space alien that has been beamed down into your body, then get curious about what you feel. What does this anger/anxiety/sadness actually feel like in your body? Where do you feel it most? Instead of being subsumed by the waterfall of your thoughts, try to see that waterfall from the outside. What are the thoughts that arise? Where do they come from? Are these thoughts true? Are they helping the situation?

This is your mindfulness practice in action. Be curious, but hold it lightly. Don't go down the rabbit hole of thinking here. Gently see what arises.

Nurture

Finally, take the time to be curious about what this feeling needs. How can you *nurture* yourself with compassion? In this step of RAIN, Insight Meditation teacher Tara Brach teaches us to hold a hand to our hearts and experiment with messages that help soothe that scared and hurting part of ourselves.

You can try saying to yourself: "It's okay." "It's not your fault." "You're not alone." "Trust in your goodness." Sometimes it's helpful to bring into your heart an unconditionally loving figure in your life—even a spiritual figure or a pet—who can soothe that wound.

RAIN can help you move *through* your emotions—mindfully processing them rather than blocking or becoming flooded. It's a practice that becomes easier with time. Eventually it will help you recover faster and have more equanimity. Let's try it.

Practice: RAIN Meditation

RAIN stands for Recognize, Allow or accept, Investigate, and Nurture with compassion. Find a comfortable, safe place to relax. Then either follow the script here or find the audio-guided RAIN meditation at http://www.raising-goodhumansbook.com.

With eyes closed and spine tall, take a deep breath in and let out a sigh. Take another deep breath in and let out a sigh. Feel the in-breath as it journeys all the way in. Feel the out-breath as it flows all the way out. Allow your muscles to soften and settle with your exhales.

Bring to mind a recent time when you experienced a difficult emotion. Make it a real event but not something traumatic in nature. As you recall the event and your difficult feelings, allow the scene to play through your mind like a video. Bring yourself to the place where you most feel the challenging emotion.

The first step in this meditation is to **recognize** *the emotion and the many forms that it takes. Be curious here about how the emotion is affecting you. Notice where you sense it in your body. Keep your breath flowing in and out. Notice what the emotion feels like in your belly, your chest, your shoulders, arms and hands, jaw and face. Recognize how this emotion feels without pushing away or blocking it. Silently answer this question: What is the name of this emotion? Notice this without judging, with curiosity. Continue to be aware of your in-breath and your out-breath.*

Next, **allow**. *Imagine yourself holding your difficult emotion in your arms like a baby. Imagine yourself saying to your emotion, "It's okay. It's okay that you're here. I'll take care of you," again and again. Practice to accept your difficult emotion—to embrace it. Continue to imagine yourself holding it in your arms like a baby. Continue to say to your emotion, "It's okay. It's okay that you're here. I'll take care of you." Say yes to the sensations that arise.*

The third step is to **investigate** *the nature of your feeling. Be curious about it. Ask your feeling gently, "Where did you come from?" Be curious about what arises. What are the thoughts that show up? Where do the thoughts come from? Are these thoughts true? Are they helpful? What happened in your body and your breath as your difficult feeling arose? Investigate your feeling so that you can understand it better.*

When you're ready, move on to the final step in the RAIN meditation: **nurture** *with compassion. Self-compassion begins to arise naturally when we recognize that we are suffering. To do this, try to sense what the wounded, frightened, or hurting place inside you needs most, and then offer nourishing messages. Does it need words of reassurance? Of forgiveness? Of companionship? Of love? Experiment and see which intentional gesture of kindness most helps to bring comfort. Try offering, "I'm here with you." "I'm sorry, and I love you." "It's not your fault." "Trust in your goodness."*

Try gently placing your hand on your heart or cheek; alternatively, try envisioning being embraced by warm, radiant light. If it feels difficult to offer yourself love, bring to mind a loving being—a spiritual figure, family member, friend, or pet—and imagine that being's love flowing into you.

When you're ready, bring your awareness back more fully to your breath. Feel your in-breath. Feel your out-breath. Then start to expand your awareness to notice feelings in your body, sounds, and the temperature of the room.

After you practice this meditation, take some time to move slowly and see how you feel. Take a moment to write down your reflections in your Raising Good Humans *journal: What was your response to RAIN? Did it help? Which parts were difficult and why?*

RAIN is not a "one-and-done" practice. Rather, consider it a tool for life. It can help you manage life's inevitable difficulties and, over time, recover from them more easily.

Taking care of our difficult feelings on a regular basis may be one of the most significant practices in this book, so please *don't just read over this section and avoid actually practicing!* Practice has the power to completely transform the most important relationship you have in your life: your relationship with yourself.

Although it's uncomfortable initially (and boy, oh boy do we want to avoid discomfort!), I urge you to *practice.* It's truly an act of bravery to sit with your shadow—the feelings you'd rather not have at all. But when you do, you'll find there's a kind of freedom on the other side. You're no longer imprisoned by your difficult emotions. With the knowledge that you have a process for taking care of them, you can move through the world with more confidence.

As we start to take care of our difficult feelings in a healthy way, our children will see that too. (Remember living what you want your kids to learn?) As we practice taking care of our own feelings, our kids will learn this healthy response from us.

Now that you have some tools to take care of your own difficult feelings, let's look at how to help your child with hers.

Helping Children Through Difficult Feelings

Scrolling through social media a while back, I saw a picture of a celebrity dad standing with other adults in a circle around his preschool-age daughter. She was on the floor, kicking wildly and clearly upset. He shared about how they were letting her have her tantrum and standing around her to keep her safe. Yes, she was on the dirty floor of a public place. Yes, strangers gawked and judged. But rather than give in to social pressure, he wisely gave his child space to release her emotions.

While I've long forgotten the name of the celebrity, I remember the sense of gratitude I felt at the powerful message he was sending: *it's okay for children to cry.*

Expect and Accept Strong Emotions

Just like adults, children get flooded by strong emotions. In fact, because the prefrontal cortex doesn't fully develop until children are in their early twenties, they are more prone to becoming flooded by strong emotions. This is an inevitable part of childhood, so as parents we need to *expect* and *accept* children's difficult emotions. Just like adults, when kids block and repress emotions, those feelings pop out in potentially destructive ways, like exploding at a sibling. Let's agree that we don't want that. So just as we practice to accept our own emotions, we must seek to accept our children's emotions and help them to accept their emotions as well.

Yes, well, we may agree that we don't want to teach our children the repression that we learned, but do we *really* feel okay about our children feeling anger or sadness? Often we feel so uncomfortable with their strong emotions that our instinct is to "fix" it right away. We distract them with toys or screens. We tell them, "Don't cry." We say, "You're okay." When we practice accepting and allowing children to have difficult feelings, instead of fixing them, our modus operandi changes. Now our work becomes taking care of our own discomfort—because there's nothing to change or fix for the child.

What does this mean? What does not fixing look like in action? It may look like the example of the celebrity letting his daughter tantrum (safely) in a public place. It may mean not shutting your child in his room when he's having a cry. It means taking a break from grocery shopping and leading your child outside to cry out her disappointment at not getting sugar cereal. It means reminding your child, "It's okay to have anger" and "It's okay to feel sad."

Does this sound like strange parenting advice? The truth is that emotional expression is healthy. Just like us, our children need to *feel it to heal it*. They may need to talk, yell, or cry. When we come from a place of *expecting* these inevitable strong emotions, we don't suffer the pain that comes from the knee-jerk reaction of denying this healthy expression. The thought, *They shouldn't feel like this* is the second arrow that creates much of the suffering felt by us and our children.

Crying Isn't a Bad Thing

Many parents will do anything to get their children to stop crying: scold, bribe, plead, send the child to his room. But the truth is that children need to cry. Sometimes they need to cry a lot. As a mom who found it *very* difficult to hear my daughter cry, I'm here to tell you that accepting this reality will make the road much smoother for you. Her crying used to make me want to crawl out of my skin, but I eventually realized that this was my work, not her problem. It took me a while to see that if we allow the feelings to flow and release, they don't cause half as much difficulty.

Don't tell children not to cry. Crying is a cathartic release for all children, and when they are done, they feel better. Phrases aimed toward boys like "Don't be a mama's boy" or "Be a man" may seem relatively harmless, but such words tell boys that they can't show their feelings. When boys are told to be strong and push away their emotions, it stunts healthy emotional development. Allow yourself to release feelings though tears, and model the normality of crying by not apologizing for it. Teach both boys and girls that crying is a healthy process that helps us feel better.

Accept Emotions, Limit Behavior

Often crying is easier to accept than anger, which often comes with aggressive behavior. Does accepting anger mean accepting destructive or harmful behavior? Of course not. We can practice accepting the emotions, but we can (and should) prevent violent behavior. We can model and teach healthier ways to express the energy of anger.

Talk with your child about ways to take care of anger preemptively, outside of the upset moment. You might offer a special blanket or soft toy, give her a corner where she can sit to draw or rip up paper, or allow her to jump on a mini trampoline. But remember that modeling taking care of your own anger is by far the most effective practice. If you yell and fly into a rage when you're triggered, how can you expect something different from your child?

Tools to Help Children with Strong Emotions

Once we have established the foundational belief that all feelings are acceptable, we can become helpers and coaches, modeling for our children how to take care of their strong feelings. When those strong feelings come up, our own first step is to get centered ourselves and notice any emotions and old stories that have been triggered by their big feelings. We can check in and ask, "Am I able to help my child now? Do I need to take a moment to calm down and reduce my reactivity?"

If you're in a relatively healthy, stable place, then you can be a good helper for your child. Remember, it's better to take a break than to lose it.

Tolerating Tantrums

Tantrums are children's way of expressing their frustration. If your child is having a full-on temper tantrum, there's not much you can do to help except stay present, keep him safe, and prevent him from hurting people or damaging objects. This can be truly challenging to do because tantrums might trigger your own big emotions. Use the tools we discussed in chapter 2 to take care of yourself and calm your triggers.

If you are able to stay present, practice staying grounded in your body, breathing, and accepting your child's big feelings. When you do this, it sends your child some wonderful messages. It tells him, "I see you. I hear you. It's okay for you to have these feelings. I'm here for you. You are safe." When your child feels safe and not abandoned, his big feelings will pass more quickly. And it tells him, "I love you no matter what you feel," demonstrating your *unconditional* love. Your silent presence is a powerful response.

When your child's done with his tantrum, support him with your physical presence. Offer hugs, snuggles, and back rubs. These loving gestures help him internalize those messages of safety and okay-ness, helping him bounce back sooner.

The following exercise is one to do when your child is having a tantrum. Read it carefully so that you have a sense of what to do when the time comes. You might even write down the basics on an index card to keep with you as a handy reminder.

Practice: Staying with a Tantrum

Staying present through a tantrum is hard work, but it has many rewarding benefits for your relationship with your child. It shows your unconditional love.

Here's how: Do not send your child to her room or isolate her. Instead, stay with your child. Get as close as you feel comfortable, keeping her safe and keeping objects and others safe from her. Sit or get down low to be at your child's level.

Notice your own sensations and thoughts. Are you starting to get tense? If so, take deep, slow breaths with long exhales to calm down your stress response. Notice if you have feelings of wanting to escape. If you can, stay and be curious about these feelings. Acknowledge them, and focus your attention on slow, calm breathing. You may notice embarrassment (especially if you're in public) or anger arise. Acknowledge those feelings, then refocus on staying with your child and breathing deeply and slowly. Practice relaxing your body.

Say to yourself, "I am helping my child," reminding your nervous system that your child is not a threat. Don't pressure yourself to have the right words. Remember that staying present is enough. As you practice staying nonreactive in this challenging moment, you are building your ability to do so again in the future. Remember that you are telling your child, "I see you. I hear you. It's okay for you to have these feelings. I'm here for you no matter what. You are safe."

As the tantrum subsides, offer hugs and closeness. Don't rush to the next thing. Move slowly and allow time for recovery.

Notice how staying with a tantrum can shift your child's response and recovery time. When you are able to sit mindfully with a tantrum, congratulate yourself! It's *hard*, and it's a big parenting win. Simply riding out this intense emotional expression is a big step in healing for both of you.

Tell a Story

When something scary and upsetting happens, children often need help processing their emotions. Their brains have become flooded by the emotions, so one way to bring the prefrontal cortex—home of our verbal, language-based processing abilities—back online is to tell the story of what happened. In *Parenting from the Inside Out* (2014), Daniel Siegel and Mary Hartzell discuss narrative as a tool for integrating the whole brain. Telling your child the story of an experience can help him process both the events and the emotions he is feeling in a healthy way.

I experienced the power of storytelling firsthand when I was on vacation with my daughters. We had recently arrived at my parents' house after a six-hour car ride when we got word that my grandfather had a fall. My parents had to leave right away to help. Abruptly, my husband, girls, and I found ourselves in my parents' house alone. Plans were changing by the hour as my grandfather's health updates came in.

My oldest daughter, who was nine years old at the time, became emotionally unsettled. She got angry about plans changing and started crying. She got into the shower, crying, and I could hear it escalating from outside the bathroom. When she got out still crying, I came in and wrapped my arms around her toweled, wet body. I started to tell the story of our vacation from her point of view, starting with us leaving the house. I told the story all the way up to that moment, adding details and feelings.

My husband and I were both surprised to find her calming down. She listened raptly to the whole story. It truly helped her. She stopped crying and was able to go on with the day.

If your child is not in a full-scale tantrum or rage, storytelling can be a powerful tool to help him process what has happened. You can tell the story, or you can prompt your child to tell you the story. Often children may tell and retell the story of an experience they need to process. Allow this repetition and be a mindful listener. You can also tell the story using puppets, dolls, or stuffed animals to act out the behaviors and feelings, as child therapists sometimes do. Storytelling helps children be able to go on with their day in a healthy, balanced way.

Taking Care of Difficult Feelings

Big emotions like anger, fear, and sadness are an inevitable part of life for both parents and kids. The more we accept and allow our feelings, the more easily we can let them pass, avoiding the suffering that comes from resistance. Pushing away our feelings may be our cultural and familial inheritance, but this is a pattern that we *can* shift and change over time. When we are able to recognize, accept, investigate, and nourish mindfully our own big feelings, then we will be able to be a grounding presence for our children in their own times of need.

When I look around at the difficulties in the world, it seems that most stem from people being unable to take care of their difficult feelings. We can start to turn this pattern around in our own families, changing things for generations to follow.

In the next chapters, we're going to look at how to communicate more effectively with our children. You'll learn how to talk to cultivate cooperation and how what you say can hinder connection. As we move into these chapters, remember that your mindfulness practice is the foundation for inside-out change. Continue to practice and grow your self-awareness and your ability to be truly present with your children.

What to Practice this Week

- Sitting Meditation or body scan meditation for five to ten minutes, four to six days per week

- Loving-Kindness practice four to six days per week

- TIPI practice

- RAIN meditation

- Experiencing Yes vs. No

- Staying with a tantrum (if applicable!)

PART II

RAISING KIND, CONFIDENT KIDS

CHAPTER 5

Listening to Help and Heal

"When you talk, you are only repeating what you already know. But if you listen, you may learn something new."

— Dalai Lama

Just as I was sitting down to write these pages, my daughter burst into the room, wildly distraught.

"Mommy! I told her but she won't make the house the way it's supposed to be! And then she took the pieces!"

Oh boy, here we go. My response in a moment like this could either escalate or deescalate the crisis. An unskillful response might unwittingly send a host of harmful messages. But a skillful response could help move me toward that elusive holy grail of parenting—where my daughter can manage her *own* difficult emotions.

What do I say? can be such a tough question. While mindfulness is the essential foundation that helps us become more grounded, it's not enough. Our choice of words makes a *huge* impact on our day-to-day life as parents. So we want to make sure that we are conscious of what we say, not just repeating the same old lines that were used on us as children. That's one way that harmful generational patterns are passed down. This chapter gets us started with that second wing to help us fly: skillful communication.

It's easy to be skillful in the happy moments. Not so much when someone has a problem. Conflicts in relationships are the result of each party trying to get his or her own needs met. The way our children go about meeting their needs may interfere with how we meet our needs, and vice versa. For instance, sometimes my child may have a problem that doesn't bother me at all, and sometimes the opposite is true. So before we answer "What do I say?" we have to know who has which problem. This is a job for the mindful inquiry you've been practicing.

A Mindful Approach to Problems

Bringing mindfulness to challenging moments sounds great, you might be thinking, *but my daughter is currently tormenting her little brother! How does beginner's mind and empathy help that?* In fact, problems and conflicts are ideal places to practice curiosity and empathy. Normally, we go into these situations with preconceived notions about who is at fault. We tend to only look at what's wrong with a child's behavior. However, making fewer assumptions can really help. You'll solve problems more effectively and compassionately when you understand that kids are simply trying to meet their needs (usually unskillfully and immaturely, but isn't that the definition of being a kid?).

This week, when there are moments of friction between you and your child, I want you to start to ask yourself two questions:

What are the *needs* that my child is trying to meet?

Who *owns* this problem?

For instance, when your child leaves a backpack in the middle of the hallway, *you* are the one who has the problem. It's not a problem to your child. It's *your* need to enjoy a tidy home that is not being met. Other times, your child might have an issue—an argument with a friend at school, for instance—that is not your problem. His argument doesn't affect your life much at all, but your child's need for connection and friendship is not being met. Start to notice whose needs aren't being met.

What I say next may be challenging and liberating all at once. Ready? *You don't have to solve or fix all of your child's problems.*

What? Isn't that what being a "good" parent is all about? No. In fact, if you take on and solve all of your child's problems, it never gives him the opportunity to come up with solutions himself. It's like a vote of no confidence in his abilities.

It's true that when children are helpless infants, we should endeavor to solve all of their problems. However, as they grow, our role changes. Instead, we shift toward becoming mentors, *helping them* solve their problems. Soon you'll learn the communication skills you need to do that. For now, work on shifting away from the mindset that you have to fix every problem for your child.

Start to ask yourself, *Whose problem is it?* If your child has a problem, think of yourself as a *helper* rather than the one who has all of the solutions and answers. This can be wonderfully freeing, because in all honesty you *don't* have all of the answers. Take that weight off your shoulders!

Practice: Who Has a Problem?

Practice slowing down and pausing before you respond to your child. Ask yourself the question: Whose problem is it?

When your child has a problem, think of yourself as an empathetic helper rather than a problem solver. What is your child needing? How can you help your child meet her needs in a better way? Bring beginner's mind (from chapter 1) and curiosity to the situation rather than judgment.

When we can look at conflicts without judgment, we can respond more thoughtfully. If I can see that my daughter (not me) has a problem, it gives me a sense of remove and objectivity about the situation that deescalates my response.

It can be challenging to let your children "own" their own problems and step back a bit, but it's so important. In her book *How to Raise an Adult* (2015, p. 89), Julie Lythcott-Haims shares the problems with doing too much for your kids with some striking research results: "Students with helicopter parents were less open to new ideas and actions and more vulnerable, anxious, and self-conscious. A student with 'hovering' or 'helicopter' parents is more likely to be medicated for anxiety and/or depression." Clearly, doing too much for our kids can have disastrous consequences.

As a parent, you may feel social pressure, peer pressure, or even familial influence to make sure your child doesn't experience challenges and difficulties. In my parent coaching practice, I teach my clients to use the mantra

"Not my problem" to help them step back a bit when they are overinvolved in fixing every problem for their children. The key here is to practice the self-awareness (your mindfulness helps with this) to know yourself and discover how you might need to balance your tendencies.

How Listening Heals

How do we help when our children have problems? When my daughter was two years old, she started having intense tantrums, often several times a day. My husband and I saw her as a ticking time bomb that could explode at any moment. The anxiety and stress were getting to me. How to cope? I had to learn to ground myself and to listen.

Start with Groundedness and Self-Compassion

First, I had to deal with my stress response. Could I keep my cool in the face of her intensity? Oftentimes, the answer was no. So I had to "get gone" to take care of my anger. Yelling only makes a hard situation worse, so getting some space from the situation to calm down helped. It didn't feel great to leave her when she was upset, but it was better than erupting into a mommy tantrum. I learned that when your child is in a safe place, sometimes temporarily leaving can be the more skillful choice.

When I was able to stay calm, I had yet another problem. The words I said triggered a whole other round of toddler screaming! Although mindfulness was helping me calm down and stay present, it turned out that I had inherited a way of speaking that triggered *resistance* in my daughter. What I said actually made things *worse*, not better, but I didn't know how to communicate more skillfully. So I set out to learn. In these next few chapters, I'll share with you the communication tools that I learned that helped to transform my daughter's outright resistance into willing cooperation.

A caveat: as you learn these more-effective ways of communicating with your child, remember to practice self-compassion and let go of self-judgment. I know firsthand how frustrating it is to realize that the way you've been communicating could be damaging your relationship. Remember your mindfulness foundation. Your mindfulness practice will give you the space and clarity you need to make changes with a healthier, less judgmental attitude. Shame and blame are not good teachers—not for your child, and not for you. Bring compassion to your learning, and remember that you are not alone—we all struggle.

Listen to Cultivate Connection

Relationships are built on connection, and connection is developed through our interactions—through communication. Fundamentally, we all want to be seen and heard, especially in our closest relationships. Unfortunately, it's often in our closest relationships—including with our children—that we tend to withdraw our attention. It might be because we are on autopilot or in "doing" mode, getting things done, or on our way out the door. Or maybe it's the phone in our hands. So we only listen with a tiny fraction of our attention. That's why your mindfulness meditation is a foundational practice. Children need us to really *be* there—body, mind, and spirit—not just telling them to hurry up and put on their shoes. As Thich Nhat Hanh said during a retreat I attended in 2003:

"When you love someone, the best thing you can offer is your presence. How can you love if you are not there?"

Every time your child talks to you, he wants to make a connection. And every time he wants to connect, think of the act as a bell of mindfulness—a reminder to pause and listen with all of your attention. To turn the phone off, put it down, and practice being fully present with your child. Or to tell him that you aren't able to listen right now.

When we practice listening mindfully—with our focused, nonjudgmental attention—we can truly understand what is going on for our children. When we listen like that, our children feel seen and heard.

Listening attentively is the gold standard for helping others when they have a problem. It helps them clarify and resolve their problem through talking it out. Sometimes listening is all it takes to find a solution! We've shown that we're really present, so our kids feel understood. They want us to accept them exactly as they are, uncomfortable feelings and all. To feel accepted is to feel loved, which heals many problems.

If we are listening to their problem with compassion, it does *not* mean that we condone their choices. Instead, it simply demonstrates that we accept them and their feelings (not necessarily their behavior).

When your child has a problem, listening with your full attention can be like magic. When you do this, you communicate so much without ever saying a word. Try saying less and listening more this week!

Practice: Mindful Listening

Make it a practice to stop talking and simply listen with your full attention. Think of it as a mindfulness practice, so that you can be fully present when your child is talking to you.

What are some ways to be fully present?

- *Put the phone and other distractions away so that you are not tempted to check them.*

- *After putting away intrusions, focus your body language toward your child. Turn your body in her direction and shift your gaze toward her. If she is sharing something uncomfortable, she may not want to make eye contact, and that's okay. Sit side by side.*

- *Use your mindfulness skills to notice when your mind is wandering into the past or into the future, is judging, or is planning a response. Instead, practice to simply be still and listen to what your child is saying. What does your child want? What happened? What is she feeling?*

Simply listening attentively, with your mind and body focused on your child, will forge a stronger connection. Give it a try and find out how helpful you can be without even uttering a word!

Taking a week or so to focus on less speaking and more listening will shift things for your relationship. You'll find yourself interrupting the old habit of solving everything and instead being more observant and curious. Best of all, your child will be able to feel the difference.

What Not to Say

Listening is one big part of building a stronger connection between us and our children. Letting go of our impulse to solve every problem is another big part. After that, *what do we say?* We can't just stay silent forever, and some responses are better than others.

First, let's look at the kind of words that are *not* helpful.

Let's imagine that your child has run over to you from the sandbox, clearly upset. "Reilly stole my bucket! She used to like me, but now she went somewhere else, and she's being mean to me. I hate this playground!" What do you say?

If you are like most of us, your response might sound like one of these:

"Oh honey, I'll bet Reilly still likes you."

"Sometimes things like this happen. Don't be so soft."

"If you shared more, then you'd still have your friend."

"Why don't you nicely ask Reilly to give it back?"

"You're fine. Do you want a snack?"

Sound familiar? Chances are, you've heard yourself or other parents responding to children in some of these ways. Now, let's imagine instead that *you* are on the receiving end of these responses. Instead of the bucket-and-sandbox scenario, imagine that your longtime friend Reilly isn't giving back a jacket she borrowed and has been giving you the cold shoulder. You go to your partner upset and wanting to talk about it—and this is what your partner says:

"Oh honey, I'll bet Reilly still likes you."

"Sometimes things like this happen. Don't be so soft."

"If you shared more, then you'd still have your friend."

"Why don't you nicely ask Reilly to give it back?"

"You're fine. Do you want a snack?"

No, I'm not fine, and I don't want a snack! Yikes. How can anybody be so insensitive? Yet this is the way we talk to children a lot of the time. Most of us were not taught skillful ways to respond to someone who has a problem. None of those responses acknowledge the person's feelings. They're all unhelpful because they send a message of nonacceptance.

If we say something like, "If you shared more you'd still have your friend," we stop the conversation with our blame and judgment. If we say, "Sometimes things like this happen. Don't be so soft," we are denying how the person feels. If we try to help the person "fix" the problem, saying, "Why don't you nicely ask Reilly to give it back?" then we are skipping over acknowledging how the person feels, which is terribly irritated.

The worst part is that all of these responses create rupture in our relationships, and it's our *connection* to our children that forms the foundation of cooperation.

Barriers to Communication

In the Mindful Parenting course, we call the type of responses discussed above "barriers" because they generally stop the flow of communication between parent and child. Children find it hard to open up and listen when we throw up these barriers.

Barriers to communication:

- Blaming

- Name calling

- Threatening

- Ordering

- Dismissing

- Offering solutions

Some examples:

Blaming: "You just don't want to do the work."

Name calling: "Don't be such a baby. You're a big boy now."

Threatening: "If you're not nice, they won't want to play with you."

Ordering: "Stop doing that!"

Dismissing: "I'm sure it's fine. Let it go."

Offering solutions: "Why don't you..."

These barriers communicate nonacceptance of the other person's thoughts and feelings. Some of them send a message that the other is wrong for having feelings. Some take the responsibility for solving the problem away from the child, acting as a vote of no confidence in their competence.

Let's take another look at the situation with Reilly. Here are the communication barriers in action:

Blaming: "If you shared more you'd still have your friend."

Name calling: "Don't be so sensitive."

Threatening: "If you're not nice, they won't want to play with you."

Ordering: "Don't say that. Just go over and make friends."

Dismissing: "You're fine. Do you want a snack?"

Offering solutions: "Why don't you just nicely ask Reilly to give it back?"

None of these responses are particularly empathetic or helpful. Variously, these responses send the message that the child is at fault, her feelings don't matter, or she's incompetent.

Change Isn't Easy

Are you recognizing any of your own communication patterns in the previous section? I certainly did as I learned about this. I used threatening, blaming, and even name calling far more than I'd realized. It can be frustrating and disappointing to learn that some of your communication patterns are unhelpful. But remember that you don't consciously choose unskillful language. The way you communicate has a lot to do with your culture and family history. Unless we make a conscious effort to change how we talk, we repeat familial and cultural patterns. You are not to blame!

Now that you are aware of these communication barriers, you may be eager to cut them out right away. However, you have to become *aware* of when you are using them. The honest truth is that it will take some time to stop. You will most likely continue to use the barriers while you are learning to recognize them *and even afterward*. I still use them sometimes! Simply becoming aware of when you use the barriers is a big win.

Learning to make changes like this requires our practice of self-compassion. We are mistake-making human beings. Even as our awareness grows, we will still make mistakes. Yet, to the degree that we can shift away from these unskillful communication patterns, our relationship with our children will improve.

How to be Helpful Instead

Let's head back to the sandbox, where your child said, "Reilly stole my bucket! She used to like me, but now she sits somewhere else, and she's always being mean to me. I hate this playground!" What should you say in response?

Remember that when our children come to us with a problem, they want to be heard, understood, and accepted. We can demonstrate that we hear them through *reflective* listening—reflecting back the content and the feelings behind what they said. You could say something like:

"Oh, honey, you're really feeling bad! It's no fun on the playground at all right now."

This acknowledges what's going on and opens the door for the child to talk a little more. You're now accepting the child's feelings. This kind of empathetic response is sometimes called "active listening." It's also called "emotion coaching," because it helps children learn to regulate their own emotions.

How does this feel on the receiving side? Let's imagine again that Reilly is your friend who's giving you the cold shoulder. You're feeling bad and go to your partner to talk. Instead of responding with, "I'm sure it's fine," your partner says, "Oh, honey, that stinks! This is really bothering you." How would you receive each of these responses?

Reflective Listening in Action

When someone has a problem and is upset, reflective listening asks us to guess and put a name to what that person is feeling. Remember how the lower brain is largely responsible for feelings? When our children are upset, the emotional brain has taken over. When we give a neutral label to the feeling, it helps bring our children's upper brain—largely responsible for logic, self-control, language, and decision-making—back into the picture.

Practice: Reflective Listening

Pay attention mindfully.

Hear the facts and the underlying feelings.

Respond with your understanding.

Express empathy.

Your primary job is to pay attention mindfully. Focus your mind and body on your child. Listen for the facts and feelings in what he is saying. When it's time to respond, share your understanding with your child. This lets him know that you're listening.

If your response was accurate, then your child will feel understood and will have gained insight into his problem. Even if you give an off response (you guessed his feelings and you were wrong) it can still help your child clarify what he is feeling and thinking. If your "guess" doesn't feel true, your child can (and will) correct it, and the two of you can go from there.

Reflective listening can be as simple as reflecting back "Ow! That really hurt," instead of "It's okay, don't cry," to a child who skinned his knee. Or it can turn into a more complex "peeling the onion" situation where the ultimate problem is revealed after working through many levels. Take this example:

A seven-year-old comes home from school and says, "I don't want to go to school tomorrow. Not tomorrow and not ever!"

Parent: "You don't want to go to school anymore."

Son: "No, I don't. Besides, I don't want to see Mason in the playground ever again."

Parent: "You sound worried about Mason."

Son: "He always makes fun of me because I don't know any of the characters in Teenage Mutant Ninja Turtles. All the kids play that game and I can't because I don't know the characters. It's not fair that I don't get to watch it."

Parent: "You wish you could watch that show."

Son: "Yeah! All the other kids know the show, and they don't play with me because I don't know it."

Parent: "Sounds like you're feeling left out."

Son: "It used to be so much better when Oliver was in my class. We loved to just hang out and draw during recess. It sucks that he had to go to another school."

Parent: "You miss Oliver."

Son: "Recess was so much better with him there. But sometimes Lucas wants to play. He's pretty cool, and Mason leaves us alone when we hang out by the tree. I could see if he wanted to play tomorrow. And I could bring my Star Wars guy! Can I bring it to school tomorrow?"

Parent: "Sure, honey."

Instead of dismissing or using the other barriers, this parent reflected back to her child, allowing the child to work out the problem on his own. Sometimes when we use reflective listening, our children feel really heard and accepted, and the story keeps "unpeeling," like this one. This child resolved his own problem by talking it out. If the parent had said, "Forget it. You have to go to school tomorrow," right away, she never would have learned what was really bugging her child.

John's Story

Harper had come home from school disgruntled about a girl who was giving her bad looks. She ranted about how mean this girl was. I asked Harper how she reacted to the dirty looks, to which she replied that she frowned back. I asked her if that helped. Harper said no.

Trying to break the negative thinking, I asked her to tell me something she likes about the girl (I was trying to "fix" the problem). "Is she a good drawer? Do you like her hair, shoes?"

I recommended that my daughter say something nice to the girl as soon as she sees her the next Monday at school.

Tuesday, when I picked up Harper from school, I saw a dark look in her eyes. I asked how school was and she broke down in a puddle of tears. This time I remembered reflective listening and said, "I am so sorry you are hurting. It's hard to start at a new school. I know it hurts." I let her cry and tell me how awful and mean the other girl in class is, and didn't try to correct her. I just held her.

I asked her a week later how things were going with this girl in her class. She said, "Fine."

Let's look at another example. Imagine that your five-year-old is resisting going to bed. She's antsy. She declares, with fervor, "I'm not going to bed tonight!" *Uh-oh*, you think. But you remember to acknowledge what's going on for her and reflect back:

Parent: "Sounds like you really don't want to go to sleep."

Daughter: "It's too scary to turn off the lights. I can't sleep."

Parent: "The darkness scares you."

Daughter: "Yeah. When it's dark it looks like there's a snake in the closet!"

Parent: "Oh my gosh, that sounds scary! No wonder you don't want to go to bed." [Offering a hug.]

Since the parent has listened, he now understands what's going on and can help effectively. In this case, the parent turns off the light and lies in the bed, noticing the shape of the clothes hanging. "Hmmm… those clothes do look like a snake. Let's make sure the closet door is closed." Notice that that is helping to solve the problem. As you learn these tools, remember to walk the middle path between extremes.

Reflective listening also works with infants and preverbal children. Imagine your baby is crying. You might say, "Don't cry. Hush. It's all right," sending the message that the baby's feelings are unacceptable.

Instead, you could say, "Oh, you're really upset. Let's see what's going on." This acknowledges the baby's reality. You've recently fed her, so you check the diaper, and yep. "This yucky diaper doesn't feel very good at all, does it?" Again this acknowledges what is going on for the child and how she might feel. The words show acceptance, while the unskillful "don't cry" language doesn't. Your soothing voice and empathetic face also acknowledge her reality and let you connect emotionally. And when you do this with your baby, you practice skillful language that you'll take into the future with your child.

Problems with Reflective Listening

As you start to use this new tool of reflecting back what your child is feeling and experiencing, you'll probably make some mistakes. The most common is trying to listen empathetically when you are simply not in a good place to listen. You may be frustrated and irritated by your child, or tired and overwhelmed.

If you aren't feeling up to listening, then be direct and honest about that. "I'm not feeling ready to listen to you right now. Can we talk about this in a little while?"

Other common reflective-listening errors include:

- **Echoing,** or repeating back exactly what your child said to you. This can irritate your child and can lead to more conflict. Instead, interpret it in a way that shows you really heard.

- **Exaggerating or minimizing feelings.** If your child is *really* angry and frustrated, and you say to her, "You're a little bit disappointed about the game being canceled," your child may not feel like you heard her.

- **Starting each feedback with the same phrase**, such as constantly repeating, "What I hear you saying is…" I did this when I was originally learning this skill and got called out on it by my daughter more than once!

- **Reflective listening to** *everything* **that your child says.** Remember about silent listening? Silence or other simple acknowledgments are better suited to many situations. Reflecting back is a great way to help *when your child has a problem.*

Reflective listening is a skill that takes attention and practice. At first you may be very conscious that you are using a new "method" *and* that you are unskilled. Don't worry, expect that. Practice really helps! You can practice in real life at home, and you can also practice at work. You can even formulate your own reflective listening responses in your head when you overhear other parents at the playground. The more you work at reflective listening, the more naturally it will come—and the more skilled you will become.

Remember, reflective listening is a great tool to use *when your child has a problem.* In the next chapter, you'll learn what to do when *you* have a problem.

Listening Strengthens Relationships

Responding to our children skillfully starts with a large dose of mindfulness: discerning what's really happening in this moment, what the feelings and thoughts in yourself and the other person are, and who has a problem right now. If you are distracted, overstressed, or in autopilot to-do list mode, chances are strong that your response will miss the mark. The primary step to effectively solve any problem is to be *present*—to really listen to, see, and hear your child without the judgmental thoughts that like to pop up. When you are grounded, clear, and present, you can see who has a problem and how you can help.

Therefore, stick to your mindfulness practices—these are your essential foundation. Beyond that, *observe* the communication barriers in action. Notice them in yourself, in your family, and in others. Notice how people respond to the barriers. *Practice* the skill of reflective listening. It's okay if you're awkward initially. If this was not the kind of communication modeled for you as a child, then remind yourself that it's like learning a new language. Give yourself some grace.

We'll talk about what to do when *you* have a problem in the next chapter. You can jump right to that, but I encourage you to take some time to practice what you've learned in this chapter first. These skills build on one another, so it's a smart idea to take time to practice reflective listening before you take the next step.

What to Practice This Week

- Sitting Meditation or body scan meditation for five to ten minutes, four to six days per week
- Loving-Kindness practice four to six days per week
- Notice use of communication barriers
- Practice reflective listening

CHAPTER 6

Saying the Right Things

"Treat a child as though he already is the person he's capable of becoming."

—Haim Ginott

Pre-pregnancy, I was a smart, accomplished woman who got things done. Then parenting a small child brought me to my knees. Once I focused on reducing my reactivity, I was able to stay a bit calmer, which helped. But I was still saying unskillful things to my child, which caused her to resist nearly everything.

It was just a typical day at home when my daughter began to complain and resist putting on her shoes. I could feel the frustration start to rise in me. I've done difficult things in the past. *I can do this and hold myself together!* I took a deep breath in and let it out slowly, feeling my shoulders relax slightly.

Then, in my nice-mommy voice I said, "Maggie, put your shoes on. We're going outside."

It didn't work. "No! I don't want to!"

"Put your shoes on. We're going outside now."

Ka-boom! *"No!! I don't wanna!!"* Tears. Screaming.

The situation was careening downhill. My calm broke, and I started to yell. I'm not proud to say that I wrestled my daughter physically into her shoes, leaving both of us crying and miserable. What happened? My massive mommy fail started with the words I spoke. The language I used ignited her resistance (again). I ordered her around and she did *not* like that.

When You Have a Problem

In the previous chapter, we learned how to listen to help children solve their own problems. Listening is the gold standard in helping others and building connection. Mindful listening will put deposits in your "relationship bank account," so that you're building a stronger foundation of connection. That alone will motivate your child to cooperate more often.

But what about when *you* have a problem? This is the chapter from which you'll learn how to talk to your child so that you can get *your own needs* met while keeping your relationship close and connected for the long term.

Building Awareness of Your Needs

Every one of us has needs: for sleep, alone time, a peaceful environment, time with friends, healthy food, exercise, and more. But, as parents, we're often not getting these needs met. We're conditioned by society to push aside our needs in favor of our children's—especially at the infant stage. Some of us are also naturally prone to rank our needs for exercise, meditation, and time with friends behind our children's activities. If this is you, hear me clearly:

Your needs are just as important as your child's.

The answer to the problem of competing needs is not to pretend that you don't have needs, or that they don't matter, or that they can be postponed for eighteen-plus years. For a healthy, sustainable relationship that is not tinged with resentment, you must start with awareness of your needs.

What are your needs? Sometimes we're so used to denying our own needs that we forget what they are beyond the basics. Take a moment with the exercise below to see which needs require more attention:

Exercise: What Are Your Needs?

Look through the following list of basic human needs. This list isn't exhaustive, just a starting point to help build self-awareness and see what might need more attention in your life. Remember, when you live a life that includes taking care of yourself, your child learns from your example. In your *Raising Good Humans* journal, write down which of your needs requires more attention.

affection	harmony	rest/sleep
air	humor	safety
appreciation	inclusion	self-expression
beauty	independence	sexual expression
choice	intimacy	
communication	joy	shelter
community	learning	space
companion-ship	love	stability
ease	mourning	stimulation
empathy	movement/exercise	support
equality	order	touch
food	purpose	trust
freedom	respect/self-respect	warmth
growth		water

Now, think about how you can better meet the needs that have been neglected. What is one concrete action you can take—like scheduling a coffee date or booking childcare—this week? Write down your intention in your *Raising Good Humans* journal, then take action!

Modeling Healthy Boundaries

Remember how our children are wonderful at doing what we do? When we model taking care of our own needs, it teaches our children how to do that in their lives. If you're a card-carrying people-pleaser, you may have had a parent who put his or her needs last. It's time to break that unhealthy generational pattern, for your own sake and for the sake of your child. If you're going to raise good humans, you need skillful ways to let your child know that his behavior is impinging on your needs.

Children need healthy boundaries. Research has shown that children who grow up with permissive parents—who don't uphold healthy boundaries and appropriate behavioral expectations—are more likely to be more self-centered, lacking in self-regulation and impulse control, and have higher rates of drug use than other children (Shapiro and White 2014). Instead of permissiveness, we should set healthy boundaries for our own mental and emotional health, and that of our children.

Children are by definition immature. We can expect that they will inevitably annoy, disturb, and frustrate us. Kids can be thoughtless, messy, and destructive—not out of malice but simply by going about meeting their own needs. When their behavior interferes with *our* needs, we must find ways to communicate that do not cause resentment and resistance—that way, we can keep our connection (and therefore our influence) strong for the long run.

Communication Barriers

As we did in the previous chapter, let's look at what *not* to say. The same barriers apply here:

Ordering

Threatening

Advising/offering solutions

Blaming

Name-calling/judging

Dismissing

Using these methods will stop the flow of communication between you and your child, leading to resentment in the child.

The best way to understand why these are barriers is to experience them yourself. In the next exercise, I'm going to ask you to imagine what it's like to be a child with a parent who is using these barriers.

Exercise: Barriers in Action

Imagine that you are a six-year-old child. You have left your snack mess on the floor (if this is difficult, imagine yourself in a roommate scenario). You got involved in something else—a book, a puzzle, a project—and you forgot about the detritus. Imagine each of the following responses from your parent (or roommate) and write down your authentic responses from the point of view of a child. How does this language make you *feel*? Really put yourself in your kid's shoes:

"Pick that up this instant. I don't want that mess left here." (Ordering)

"If you don't pick that up right now, I'm going to take away your screen time." (Threatening)

"You know better than to leave such a mess on the floor." (Blaming)

"You're such a slob sometimes! Clean up your mess." (Name calling/judging)

"If I were you, I'd clean up your mess right after you finish." (Advising/offering solutions)

Write your reactions in your journal. It can also be helpful to read this to your partner and have him or her record a response. Use these as a starting point for conversation.

How did the kind of language in the preceding exercise make you feel? Did you want to cooperate, or did you feel some resentment? What you find may be eye opening. If you realize that your own language has been a source of resentment and resistance for your child, practice self-compassion (chapter 3). Remember, this is likely not language you consciously chose but unskillful language you inherited. You have the ability to change this. When you start to practice using more skillful language, it will become easier and more natural with time.

Ordering. Let's look at the first barrier, ordering: "Pick that up this instant. I don't want that mess left here." From the perspective of the child, it's easy to see how orders cause resentment. Children face an avalanche of orders from adults every day, and they resist being told what to do. The parent is cracking the whip and the child may want to "save face."

Threatening. The second barrier is threatening: "If you don't pick that up right now, I'm going to take away your screen time." Threatening causes a similar kind of resistance in children. They feel coerced and manipulated. In this case, the child is backed into a corner and will either resist or submit, but either way it causes resentment. While threatening may "work" in the moment, it makes the child *less* likely to voluntarily cooperate in the future.

Blaming. "You know better than to leave such a mess on the floor," "You're such a slob sometimes! Clean up your mess." Blaming and name calling are put-downs. With these responses, the parent is highlighting the mistake and implying that the child's character is in question. The child may feel guilty, unloved, and rejected. The child feels that the parent is being unfair and will often actively resist the parent's message. To cooperate (or *submit*, from the child's point of view) is to admit that the parent's words are true.

Name calling. Put-downs are deprecating and have a destructive effect on your child and on your relationship. *Your closeness and connection with your child is what makes her want to cooperate with you.* Both blaming and name calling damage that connection and should be avoided completely.

Advising and offering solutions. Do you offer a lot of solutions? "If I were you, I'd clean up your mess right after you finish." This may not feel as harsh as the other barriers, but it usually doesn't have the desired effect; it also tends to cause resentment. Have you ever been in a situation where you're ready to do something nice for someone when that person directs you to do exactly what you were about to do on your own? Your reaction was probably "I didn't need to be told." Or you may have gotten irritated because it seemed the other person didn't trust you enough to do it on your own. The problem with advising is the same problem with ordering: children don't like to be told what to do. It also sends the message that you don't trust your kid to solve the problem on her own.

Can you see how these very typical responses can cause resentment? They may have already created a pattern of resistance in your child. When you look at it from a kid's point of view, you can really see how some of these barriers are impolite and even downright rude. Yet, this way of talking with children is socially acceptable. Perhaps the biggest problem with the barriers, however, is that they are *ineffective*. This language is actually counterproductive because it leads our children to resist and resent our requests, making them *less* likely to want to cooperate.

The Problem with "You" Messages

If you look at all the unskillful language discussed above, there is a common theme: the message is all about "you"—the other person. Children experience *you-messages* as judgmental evaluations, which stokes a feeling of resentment. Think about it this way: if *my* needs aren't being met—for example, if I am tired, grumpy, and can't enjoy the living space when there's kids' stuff everywhere—this is *my* problem.

And yet, we express ourselves with you-messages, attacking our children in the process.

A Better Way to Speak

The good news is that since language and habits of speaking are *learned*, they can be unlearned. Waking up to the fact that our habitual ways and patterns are ineffective is an essential step in interrupting those old patterns and creating new, more-effective habits of speech. Please do not blame and shame yourself for speaking unskillfully. Instead, celebrate your new awareness as the start of a new pattern of mindful communication with your child.

Intention Is Transformative

We can't put up the walls of a house without a foundation. Our intentions form the foundation of our communications. To shift our language, we have to shift our *intention*.

Let's be real: in our interactions with our kids, we're usually trying to manipulate them—to *make* them do something. We need to change our way of thinking, from changing the other to expressing our own unmet needs.

This is where the mindfulness training comes in hand—to help us become more aware of what's happening under the surface. Whatever the situation, we can get *curious* about the unmet needs underneath. When we drop to this deeper level, compassion for ourselves and for our children arises. We can express ourselves with an *intention of curiosity and care*—for both ourselves and the other.

We usually come from a very different intention, however. Our unconscious mindset may be: *I don't trust you. I have to* make *you do what I want you to do.* Let's think about how your interactions might change if instead you were coming from a perspective of: *I need to make sure my needs are being met.* Because in all human interactions, we're trying to get our needs met. When we start to see this in ourselves and in our children, the blame and judgment drop away naturally.

Intention is important because if we use this new language but have the same old intention to manipulate our children, it probably won't work. They'll see right through us and resist the message as a disguised attempt to control them. If we try to just apply the "technique" without shifting to an *intention of curiosity and care*, our children feel the difference.

We've already seen that in how threats and orders reduce our children's desire to cooperate. What makes them want to cooperate? A strong connection and honest communication of your feelings about how their behavior affects your needs.

Skillful Confrontation: I-Messages

If we refrain from blaming and shaming—looking instead at how the behavior affects ourselves—our language naturally shifts to an "I" perspective. The *I-message* is a tried-and-true method of skillful communication, in which our statements generally start with "I" rather than "you." I-messages are great because they help us meet our needs without putting the child on the defensive. They also help us take ownership of our own feelings rather than implying that they are caused by our children. We can use I-messages to express our own needs, expectations, problems, feelings, or concerns to our children in a respectful way without attacking them. We can even use I-messages to express praise and appreciation more skillfully.

As we saw, our not-so-effective language of confrontation is all "you" oriented:

"**You** left a mess."

"If **you** don't stop that, then…"

"**You** should know better."

"**You** are acting like a baby."

"**You** shouldn't have done that."

But when we instead tell our children how their unacceptable behavior makes us feel, the language turns into an "I" message:

"**I** feel discouraged when I see this big mess."

"**I** don't want to race right now because I'm tired."

"**I** feel stressed when we have to hurry."

Kids receive an I-message as a statement of fact about what the parent is feeling, so it causes less resistance.

How do you use I-messages to confront difficult behaviors? Start by using your mindfulness foundation to check in with yourself: How does the situation make you feel? What thoughts and needs are you having? Are you experiencing physical sensations in the body?

Once you are aware of how the behavior affects you personally, you can share that honestly with your child. When you express with honesty and kindness what's going on for you, your child will have little to argue with. Your statement now invites empathy rather than resistance, helping your child to cooperate because she *wants* to, not because she is forced to.

For instance, think back to the child who left a snack mess on the floor. Again, imagine that you are the child. This time, the parent crouches down to your level, looks you in the eye, and says, "I feel frustrated that this is left on the floor because now I can't use and enjoy the room." How does child-you feel? How do you respond?

Thomas Gordon coined the term "I-message" and first described it in *Parent Effectiveness Training* (1970). According to Gordon, a clear I-message has three parts: a nonblameful description of the behavior, the effects it has on you, and your feelings.

Describe the behavior. Use simple statements without judgments. For example, "When your hair isn't brushed…" instead of "Your hair is such a mess!"

Describe a specific, tangible effect. What effect does it have on you? This must be on *you*, not a sibling or another person. What needs of yours are not being met? It's a tangible effect if it:

- Costs you time, energy, or money (for example, replacing cushions, mending holes, doing unnecessary errands, etc.)

- Prevents you from doing something you want or need to do (for example, getting somewhere on time, using the Internet, enjoying your living room, etc.)

- Upsets your body or senses (for example, loud noise, pain, tension)

Share your feelings. What is your honest, authentic response to this behavior? Are you disappointed, resentful, hurt, sad, embarrassed, scared?

I-messages require us to step out of the role of all-knowing parent and be *real*. They require us to mindfully look inside rather than just react to the other. They certainly require us to pause and think about the way we're going to respond.

What does an I-message look like in action?

"I told you to put away your toys now!" becomes: "With your toys all over the floor, I feel annoyed because I step on them and it hurts my feet."

"Don't kick me—that's a terrible way to act!" becomes: "Ouch! That really hurts my shins!"

"Stop that yelling!" becomes: "When you yell, I can't hear anything and I feel grumpy and frustrated."

"You are so lazy! No one cleaned this up." becomes: "I feel disappointed when I see this big mess."

Exercise: Practice Describing Without Judgment

It's often not easy to restrain the judgments from coming out of our mouths! Since our minds are constantly evaluating the world for threats, judgments will arise easily and often. That's okay. Remember, what you practice grows stronger, so let's practice nonjudgmental descriptions.

In your *Raising Good Humans* journal, practice turning the following statements into nonblameful descriptions of the behavior:

"You're so selfish!" as a child refuses to help clean up from dinner

"Don't be slobby," to a child with clothes all over the floor

"That's so rude," to a child teasing her sibling

"You always leave a mess," as a child walks away without cleaning up the toys

When we shift away from blame and judgment in our language, it naturally builds a closer connection to our children. Don't worry if this isn't easy. Even the practice of simply pausing to think about what to say will improve the way you speak.

I-messages are the most skillful means for communicating without causing resistance in our children. But they are not easy. They take skill and practice. Expect to crouch down at your child's level, make eye contact, and repeat your I-message several times.

Expect Resistance

I-messages can sometimes turn behavior around right away, but not always. If we have been in the habit of using communication barriers, our children likely won't be receptive to our I-messages, at least not initially. They're in the habit of resisting you. Think of this resistance like a train that's moving ninety miles an hour in one direction. You want to turn that train around, but it has a lot of momentum. It takes time and consistent effort to get the train to stop, turn around, and run in the other direction. But the effort is worth it, and it pays off in spades as parenting gets easier and easier over the long term.

Note that sometimes your I-messages might not work because your child's behavior is meeting a strong need. Maybe he can't think of another way to meet that need. In the next chapter, we'll dive into how to deal with these more challenging conflicts.

Troubleshooting I-Messages

You will inevitably make some mistakes as you are learning this new way of speaking. Let's look at some of the common problems you'll have with your I-messages:

You-message disguised as an I-message. Anytime you feel the urge to add the word "like" after "I feel," it's probably not a word that describes your emotions: "I feel like you're being selfish." "I feel like you're not listening to me." Simply starting a statement with "I feel" doesn't make it an I-message.

Contradictory or inauthentic feelings. Children can tell when we downplay or exaggerate how we feel, and they see it as dishonesty. For example, you see your young child running wild with a weed whacker and you downplay it with: "I feel a little bit uncomfortable because you might get hurt." Or you exaggerate your feelings: "I'm shocked and appalled that you wiggled in your seat at Grandma's house." In both cases, overshooting or undershooting your I-messages means your child will see right through it.

Leaving out the effect. Sometimes just telling your child how you feel about his behavior is enough, but if it's not working, the problem could be neglecting to explain how it *affects* you. When I say to my daughter, "I feel annoyed when you shake the table at dinner," she may not care too much. But if I include, "and I am not able to eat my food in peace," that can make a big difference.

The effect can be the hardest part of an I-message. How do you describe simple stress? I've realized that discomfort in my body, such as tense muscles, is a truly legitimate effect. For instance you could say, "When you do that high-pitched whistle in the house, I feel aggravated and stressed, and it makes my muscles tense up all around my neck so I can't relax at all!"

Stating how it affects someone else. You'll have more success when the effect is on *you*—the sender of the message. We usually make this mistake when dealing with sibling conflicts. For example you may say, "I feel so sad about what I see. Hitting hurts your little sister!" But, while it's an important message, at that moment it's just not a big motivator. Instead you could say, "I feel so sad and upset and when I seeing hitting, I can't relax for a moment or enjoy being with you!" (Then comfort the one who has been hurt.)

Your I-messages also may not be working if you are shouting them from another room. They simply won't make a difference if your intention is to shame and blame. Always remember that it is your *connection* to your child that forms the foundation for his desire to cooperate with you and help you meet your needs. So connect: stop what you're doing, get down to his level, look your child in the eyes, then share your message. Write down this mantra:

Connect, then correct.

For your confrontation to be loving and effective, come from a nonjudgmental perspective of getting your needs met, maintaining the relationship, and helping your child see the effects of his behavior.

Positive I-Messages

Before we end this session on I-messages, I want to point out that they are also a powerful tool for sending *positive* messages too. The idea is to use I-messages to be more descriptive and specific about our praise. For example, instead of "You are such a good girl helping Mommy!" you could say "I really feel good when I see you helping to clear the table." When I see my girls at the bus stop, I usually say, "I'm so happy to see you!" right away rather than peppering them with questions about the school day.

Positive I-messages are a great way to make "deposits" in your child's emotional bank account. When you focus your energy on acknowledging the positive, you build a strong connection, which helps *enormously* if you need to confront a problem behavior later.

Exercise: Craft a Positive I-Message

Let's send some appreciation to your partner, a friend, or a family member, so he or she knows how much you value him or her. Think about something that person has said or done that has made your life better. How can you describe the behavior nonjudgmentally? How did it affect your life? How did it make you feel? *Right now,* before something distracts you, take out your phone and text this person your positive I-message. Observe how it impacts your relationship for the better!

I-messages take a lot of effort upfront, but they pay off in the long run. When we parent with threats, parenting will become harder and harder over time. But when we confront our children's behavior with loving and effective communication, such as with I-messages, it actually gets easier and easier over time, because our children are used to receiving and giving respect.

Now let's look at some other ways to get our needs met without being that nasty, mean parent.

Use the Friend Filter

I-messages can be tough to conjure in a stressful moment, especially as you are first learning them. Another way to communicate more skillfully is to use what I call "the friend filter."

We bark orders at our children, blame them, threaten them, and call them names—we speak in a way we would *never* speak to our friends or our friends' children.

We give commands constantly: "Put your shoes on." "Brush your teeth." "Come over here." From our children's point of view, our orders are relentless. Our little ones chafe against all that controlling language, which act as withdrawals from the relationship bank account.

I'm not suggesting that you shouldn't make your child brush her teeth. But can you say it more skillfully? Use *the friend filter* by asking yourself: *How would I say that to a good friend?* Or better yet, *How would I say it to my friend's child?* This way of thinking can be helpful in all kinds of situations, from table manners to the playground.

It may also help you to remember to use your I-messages: "Take your shoes off the couch" turns into, "Whoa! I'm worried those shoes will mess up my couch!" "Brush your teeth," becomes "Hey kiddo, it's time to brush your teeth." Just ask yourself, *How would I say this to my friend's child?*

Another way to avoid a constant onslaught of orders is to simply set the limit with a single word, just as we might with a friend. Instead of barking the order, like, "Put on your bike helmet," you can just point to it and say, "Helmet."

Set Limits Playfully

Not only can we set limits with less severity, we can even add a dash of fun into the mix. Our attitude and energy is infectious, so if we can be a little playful, it will lighten everyone's mood and make our children less resistant to our requests. Setting limits playfully is a wonderful idea (when we can authentically manage it), and it's certainly a muscle that we can strengthen with practice.

Psychologist Lawrence Cohen writes in his book *Playful Parenting* (2001) about how play and silliness can help us nurture closer connections and solve problems. His rule? If it gets them giggling, you're doing it right.

Here are some suggestions on getting your needs met while setting healthy boundaries in a playful way:

- **Get into character.** Special Agent Mama reporting for bath duty! Or become an alien who's just arrived on Earth and ask your child (in your best alien voice), "What are these objects? Can you teach me how to clean up?" Become a cowboy, a princess, a Southern belle, and so on. Set your limits with silliness. Giggles are good!

- **Become contrary.** In a silly, exaggerated way, demand that your child do the *opposite* of what you want him to do. "Please don't get in the tub. Don't do it! You know I hate it when you're clean! Ew, you're using soap!" Sometimes children resist our limits just because they feel powerless. Exaggerating the opposite stance allows your child to have some power.

- **Use silly language or sing silly songs.** You get bonus points if you add in a dance! Try your best robot voice and beep it out like a robot: "Beep bop! Bath time!" And why talk, when you can sing? "The shoes, the shoes, it's time to put on the shooooes!" is much more fun to cooperate with than our typical orders. Try (to the tune of "My Darling Clementine"), "Oh my darling, oh my darling, it is *really* time to go! You are playing, and don't want to, but still it's time to go!"

- **Tell a crazy story.** This can be very short and really silly. "Did I ever tell you about the little blue cat who didn't stay next to his mommy in the park?" Aim for giggles and a very obvious moral to your story.

- **Become incompetent.** Kids find it hilarious when you act as though you can't do basic things. "Oh no, I forgot how to leave this park and I can't find the exit! Is it here [bumping into tree]?" "Time to brush our teeth! Wait, where are our teeth? Are they here [bringing toothbrush to ears or elbows]?" "Bedtime! I'm so tired! Let me lie down on this comfy bed [lying down on your child without hurting her]." This gets kids giggling and puts them in the responsible adult seat when they help you.

- **Use dolls, toys, or your hand as a character.** Is there a recurrent limit that you have trouble with? Act it out with dolls or stuffed animals. Follow your child's lead and allow for creative problem solving or role playing. To set a limit in the moment, you don't need a puppet, you can use your own hand as a playful character.

We yearn for a heartfelt connection with our children—one that will last through the years. If we can summon some energy to be playful instead of serious and demanding, we create that connection by bringing a sense of fun into everyday activities. We can set limits *and* have those positive, smiling moments that we envisioned when our children were just a twinkle in our eyes.

Loving and Effective Speech

It's not your fault if your habit of speaking until now has not been so skillful. Please do not blame and shame yourself or your partner for old habits of speech. We've had generation after generation of orders and threats. But now that we know better, we can do better.

You also don't have to craft perfect I-messages or an optimal robot voice to start to shift things in a positive direction. Like everything, you'll get better at these new skills with time and practice. Don't give up if you're awkward in the beginning. That's normal. Instead, play the long game and continue to practice. It's about *progress*, not perfection.

When you are able to make these skills a part of your life, you'll start to gradually see less and less resistance from your child. And unlike orders and threats, using I-messages and setting playful limits will make parenting easier over time. Why? Because your child will learn that she can trust you to treat her with respect and consideration, so she will authentically want to cooperate with you. This way of speaking develops your child's innate sense of empathy. She will come to see you as a real human with feelings and needs of your own.

I-messages and playful limits are not magic. They won't always change the behavior that's interfering with your needs. Sometimes your child's own needs are strong, and you have a conflict of needs. You'll learn how to deal with that situation in the next chapter.

You are at the beginning of learning a new language of respect, kindness, and consideration. As you start to bring this new language into your life, your child will pick up on your skillful communication and start to use it herself. While it may take a while to see this, don't worry and keep practicing! There will be a shift, bit by bit, over time—and it may make all the difference in the world.

What to Practice This Week

- Sitting Meditation or body scan meditation for five to ten minutes, four to six days per week

- Loving-Kindness meditation four to six days per week

- Notice use of communication barriers

- Practice I-messages

- Practice setting limits playfully

CHAPTER 7

Solving Problems Mindfully

"Instead of teaching children how to consider their own needs in relation to the needs of those around them... we force children to do what we want because it seems more efficient, or because we lack the energy or skill to do it differently."

—Oren Jay Sofer

I had just come out to my studio to write this when I saw my oldest daughter walking toward me saying, "Mommy, there's a conflict inside, and Daddy says I should come out and get you." In I go to find that I had just missed some big emotional outbursts. I found my youngest child in my husband's arms, crying. The girls were having trouble sharing—per usual!

In the past I might have acted like the judge and jury, passing down my decision from on high. Instead, I listened reflectively to each daughter (occasionally reminding the other not to interrupt). I summarized my understanding of both sides. Then I pulled out my Mindful Parenting judo move: I talked about the *needs* of each daughter, separate from the solutions. They both had a need for fairness! Once we figured that out, they were able to come to a resolution.

Conflicts are a normal, natural part of family life, and we should expect them frequently. In fact, research has shown that siblings have a conflict on average once an hour, and, on average, parents have a conflict with their adolescent once a day (Bögels and Restifo 2014). We have so much resistance to conflict, but when we accept that conflicts are normal, it becomes easier to let go of the irritation that arises. Remember that equation, pain x resistance = suffering? It's time to expect conflict and accept that it's an inevitable part of human relationships. We don't have to feel guilty or that it's somehow our fault when children fight or when we have a conflict with our partner. Conflict is normal.

Why? Because we all have needs, and often we go about meeting our needs in ways that interfere with someone else's needs. I may have a strong need to have some quiet time while my six-year-old has a need to jump around and let out her energy. If your child has a strong need that is interfering with your needs, that is a *conflict of needs*. Staying grounded and calm, practicing reflective listening, and using your I-messages will help you navigate through many of these situations. But what do you do when those tools aren't enough? Then, you need more nuanced conflict-resolution skills. That's what this chapter is all about.

> We've seen that meditation increases levels of well-being, resilience, and impulse control. Your sitting meditation sessions will help you lessen your stress response so that you can respond with equanimity and empathy with the inevitable problems that arise. Mindfulness meditation is the foundation of our conflict-resolution skills—helping us to respond in a way that is compassionate, thoughtful, and based on our human-to-human connection.

Traditional Conflict Resolution

What do we parents do when we need to get our children to do something, and our efforts at skillful communication aren't working? This is often when we "put our foot down" to enforce our solution. One person "wins," getting his or her needs met, and the other "loses." Depending on our parenting approach, this outcome might suit us just fine—for example, if we subscribe to an authoritarian parenting style.

Authoritarian Parenting and Conflict

In an authoritarian parenting approach, the solution to a problem is handed down from above by the parent. The parent lays down the law, and the child must obey.

Authoritarian parenting styles stem from the belief that, in order to develop properly, children need to be punished for bad behavior and be rewarded for good behavior. The goal of this approach is to teach children to comply with all parental requests. Children obey in order to avoid punishment, when the parent uses power to inflict physical or psychological suffering on the child. This may feel like a familiar and sensible approach. However, parents who use the authoritarian approach pay a high price for obedience.

If you had told me eight years ago that I would not use punishment with my children, I would have thought you were crazy. How would I have any control? I remember getting to know a new family in the neighborhood who didn't use time-outs, and I thought that they were delusional. I was *not* going to be the kind of parent who let her children run rampant. The funny thing is, I don't use punishment now and I haven't for years… and my children don't run rampant, thank you very much.

There were two problems with my former ideas about punishment: (1) I didn't realize what punishment teaches children; and (2) I didn't have a clear alternative model.

What Children Learn from Punishment

One of the biggest problems with punishment is that it doesn't actually teach our children anything helpful. The premise of the authoritarian approach is that if we punish children for misbehavior, they will see the error of their ways and want to do the right thing. But what it's ultimately teaching them is that the person with the most power wins, fair or not (which means that when they have more power, they can push their solution down on the weaker person).

Punishment causes resentment. While fear of punishment wins in the short run, in the long run, punishment makes your child less likely to cooperate because she has learned to resent her punisher—you. This anger and resentment builds up inside and erodes your close connection to your child.

Punishment can be psychologically damaging. Both physical punishment and harsh verbal punishment (yelling) can have lasting harmful effects on our children. Physical punishment, such as spanking, is hugely damaging. The evidence keeps piling up that physical punishment is associated with verbal and physical aggression; delinquent, antisocial, and criminal behavior; poorer quality of parent-child relationships; impaired mental health; and later abuse of one's own spouse and children (Gershoff et al. 2010).

Yelling isn't much better. A longitudinal study of 967 families found that harsh verbal discipline in early adolescence can be harmful to teens later, increasing risk of misbehavior at school, lying to parents, stealing, or fighting. Moreover, parents' hostility increases the risk of delinquency and fosters anger, irritability, and belligerence in adolescents (Wang and Kenny 2013). Bottom line: yelling made the behavior *worse*, not better.

Punishment makes children self-centered. Punishment focuses children on the "consequences" they suffer, rather than on the consequences of their behavior to someone else. This makes a child more self-centered and less empathetic. It teaches kids to look out only for themselves and blame others. The child may also feel wronged, so they resent making amends.

Punishment teaches children to lie. Children are incentivized to avoid punishment in the future, so they will sneak and lie to escape detection. In this way, punishment fosters dishonesty.

Punishment doesn't teach children good behavior. One of the biggest problems with the punishment approach is that children don't learn to do the right thing. They learn that if they make a mistake, they will be called "bad" and will end up hurting in some way (if they are caught). They don't learn how to account for others' feelings because they're so focused on their own suffering (from the punishment). The motivation for children is to simply *avoid punishment*. They lose many opportunities to develop their inner moral compass. Also, children will mimic our dominating behavior, learning to use their power over others who are less powerful. They don't learn to think about either their own needs or the needs of others—or how those needs might get met with fairness and respect.

Punishment makes kids less likely to cooperate. Punishment—even time-outs—erode our relationships with our children, making them *less* likely to want to help you. Because children had no choice in the solution to the conflict, they aren't motivated to follow through on the solution. Parents have to be "The Enforcer." Children then feel resentful and angry at their parents, which makes them less likely to cooperate. Your child identifies *you* as the cause of his suffering, so his anger and resentment builds.

If punishment doesn't work, then how are we to solve our problems and get our needs met? Some parents believe the answer is to let the kids make the rules. This is *permissive parenting.*

Permissive Parenting and Conflict

What if you believe that children are inherently good and that they have a deep knowledge of what's best for themselves? Or what if you're simply tired of conflict and decide to let the children do what they want? Both of these attitudes can lead you to use a permissive parenting style.

When permissive-style parents and their kids have conflicts, solutions are generally up to the child. The child "wins" and the parent "loses." With this approach, the tables are reversed and the parent can start to resent the child. Permissive parenting tends to make kids more self-centered, less able to self-regulate, and even more at risk of using drugs. While some children of permissive parents may feel psychologically more secure than those of authoritarian parents, their behavior is often more out of control (Lewis 2018).

Curiously, like children of very authoritarian parents, children of excessively permissive parents also miss out on opportunities to learn two crucial life skills: empathy and self-discipline. When children get all of their needs met at the expense of their parents, they learn to be self-centered. Because Mom and Dad never asserted their own needs, the child doesn't learn how to take others' needs into account. Without healthy boundaries, kids don't build self-restraint or self-discipline, which are at the heart of all successful endeavors. A child without much empathy or self-discipline is set up for a life of struggle.

Conflict Resolution Through Balancing Needs

Both authoritarian and permissive parenting approaches treat conflict resolution like a zero-sum game: one party wins and the other loses. One person has all of the power and the other doesn't get his or her needs meet. The big problem with these approaches is that they stay on the surface level of solutions, rather than going to the deeper level of understanding each other's needs. It is usually possible to find ways to meet each party's needs so that everyone can win.

Looking at these extremes helps us see that solving conflicts in the family is more complex than simply demanding obedience or giving kids what they want. How we resolve our conflicts reflects our deeper views about humanity, and we unconsciously transmit these to our children. Are people inherently good or are we all sinners? Is it a dog-eat-dog world where we have to fight to get our needs met? Do we always obey the one who has the most power?

Instead, let's ask this question: How do we find the middle path, where everyone can get their needs met? How can we demonstrate that, with a little more effort and understanding, there are ways for us all to win?

I believe discipline is the key, and by *discipline* I don't mean creating obedience through punishment but via teaching, mentoring, and modeling for our children. The Latin roots of the word are *disciplina*, meaning "teaching, learning, knowledge," and *discipulus*, meaning "pupil, student, follower." What method of problem solving do we want to model, with the end in mind of raising our children to be emotionally healthy, well-adjusted adults?

Understanding Parent-Child Conflicts in Terms of Needs

When our children inevitably frustrate, irritate, and annoy us with their behavior, they are trying to meet some need of theirs. If my youngest child is incessantly interrupting my conversation with my husband, her need for attention is interfering with my need to talk to my partner. How do I deal? My meditation practice keeps me grounded and less reactive. My I-message also helps: "When you keep interrupting, I feel annoyed because I can't hear what Daddy's saying." But what do I do when she continues with this behavior? How do we resolve this conflict of needs?

Most people have conflicting solutions on how to solve their shared problem and meet their needs. My daughter's solution is for me to end my conversation. My solution is for her to be quiet and let me talk. It's easy for us to get stuck on the level of solutions. However, if we can come together with the aim of getting everyone's underlying *needs* met, then the conflict can usually be resolved peacefully.

Often, once we get down to the level of needs, an obvious solution will appear. Getting there could take the form of a simple conversation during the conflict (if there's enough emotional stability), or it could require a more structured conversation later when each party has had a chance to cool down. For many small conflicts, like the one in which my daughter was interrupting me, we can talk to our children to figure out what their needs are in the moment.

Connecting During a Small Conflict

Conflict resolution starts with connection, so I turn my body toward my daughter, touch her gently on the sleeve, make eye contact with her, and give her my I-message: "When you keep interrupting, I feel annoyed because I can't hear what Daddy's saying." If she continues to interrupt, then her need is clearly very strong. So then I reflectively listen, guessing at her underlying needs: "Seems like you're worried I'm going to keep talking and forget you, and you have something *really* important to tell me." When she affirms this, I suggest a solution that meets both of our needs: "Okay, this won't take long, so as soon as I'm done talking to Daddy, I'll give you my attention. You can even gently put your hand on my shoulder so I don't forget." With this, she is satisfied and both of our needs are met.

Win-Win Problem Solving

Sometimes we have more difficult conflicts. It helps enormously in those moments to have a reliable process to resolve the problem. One very effective process is called win-win conflict resolution. Here are the steps:

Steps of Win-Win Problem Solving

1. **Identify** *needs*, not solutions.

2. **Brainstorm** as many solutions as you both can think of.

3. **Evaluate** what will meet both of your needs.

4. **Make decisions** on who will do what and by when.

5. **Check in** to see if everyone's needs have been met.

When we resolve conflicts this way, it has the inherent benefit of fairness because everyone's needs are equally important, and everyone's needs must be met. Without one party pushing its solution onto the other party, love and respect is promoted in the family instead of resentment. Here's how to make this process work:

1. **Identify needs.** Start out by writing down the needs of each party. Get it on paper so that your child can clearly see that his needs and solutions are being acknowledged. Even if you have a child who can't yet read, he will love to see his needs written out—better if it's on a really big piece of paper!

The most critical and challenging part of this step is *separating your needs from your solutions*. Often when people use the word "need" they are actually referring to solutions to an unexpressed need. For instance, your child may say, "I need to have a cell phone." This is a solution. To suss out the need underneath the child's solution, you can use the question "What will that do for you?" to clarify the needs. It's a gentle, nonpushy way of helping your child clarify his need. In this case, your child may need independence and closer connections to his friends. Once you've figured out the underlying need, write it down to acknowledge it.

2. **Brainstorm.** It's important that you encourage your child to offer his ideas first and to come up with as many ideas as possible without judging them. Write every idea down, even if it is outlandish (such as, "create a room-cleaning robot"). Your child will appreciate you taking his ideas seriously, and it's a great way to add some levity to the process! *Do not evaluate the ideas while brainstorming.* Just write them all down.

3. **Evaluate.** You can use this simple system to go through the list of ideas quickly:

✓   A checkmark for any solutions that everyone agrees on

✗   An X for any solutions that everyone does not want or isn't possible

?   A question mark for any solutions that you do not all agree on

Go down the list quickly with this system. (At this point, you will often have a fairly good idea as to what the solution will be, but keep going.) Then return to those tagged with a question mark. Check to see if they really do meet everyone's needs.

4. **Make decisions.** Discuss the solutions using I-messages and reflective listening. Come up with new solutions as needed. Once you choose a solution (or solutions), write down your plan: decide who will do what by when.

5. **Check in.** Agree to check in on the solution at a later date to see if it is still meeting everyone's needs. If everything's going well, this is a wonderful chance to remember how you all solved the problem by working together. If not, then another round of win-win might be necessary.

If this kind of problem solving is not in your repertoire, then it can seem a bit daunting initially. I recommend trying win-win for the first time with a *positive* problem.

Exercise: Win-Win Problem Solving with a Positive Problem

A great place to start bringing win-win into your life is with a *positive* problem, such as where to go on your next vacation or what to do on the weekend.

Here's how to do it: Decide on a positive decision you need to make that you want everyone's input on. Invite your children into a conversation with you, and have a big piece of paper ready. State the problem simply ("We have both days open next weekend and we'd like to decide what to do").

1. Identify your needs (for example, "I'm going to need to take care of my body with some exercise"). Ask each person what he or she will be needing ("What do you think you will be needing next weekend?"). Write everything down. *Be sure to translate their solutions into underlying needs.* Ask the question, "What will that do for you/me/us?" to suss out the underlying needs.

2. Brainstorm ideas, writing every single idea down. *Do not evaluate yet!*

3. When all the ideas are out there, use the ✓, ✗, ? system to move quickly through the list of ideas. Practice staying grounded, listening reflectively, and using your I-messages as needed.

4. Decide upon the plan that meets everyone's needs. Write out your plan, so that your child can see her ideas on paper.

5. Finally, don't forget to check in! After your weekend is over, come back to your notes and have a conversation about how it went. Did everyone get his or her needs met? This step shows that you take your child's input seriously and that her needs matter to you—making her more likely to cooperate voluntarily in the future, when the situation may be more emotionally heated.

Problems with Win-Win

If your child is used to resisting your demands and resenting the solutions that are pushed down on him from above, he may not trust that you are actually going to take his needs to heart. You're likely to have a hard time with the initial steps of this method—simply getting started and getting your kid to come to the table. Why? Remember the train going full steam in the other direction (resistance)? The same thing is happening here. It may take some discussion and convincing to get your child to participate in win-win problem solving.

Practicing win-win with positive problems before you try it with conflicts can help let your child know what's in it for him. When a conflict comes up, tell your child that you want to talk about the problem at a future time. If you haven't used win-win before, briefly explain the method and assure your child that *both* of you need to be happy with the results. Be prepared to listen reflectively! Then agree to do your win-win session at a later date. Choose a time when no one is hungry, cranky, or tired.

Another problem often arises when we slip into evaluating the ideas during our brainstorming. It's a natural habit to evaluate the ideas as they come up, but practice restraint here! It's essential to keep evaluation separate from brainstorming. Judgment stops the flow of ideas. Explain this to your kid and help him to practice restraint too.

Once you and your family have practiced win-win a number of times, this way of thinking will become shorthand for you. Your problem solving sessions will likely become shorter and more on the fly. However, in the beginning, expect it to take some time and repetition, just as with anything new we learn. It won't go absolutely smoothly, so expect some bumps. Use your skillful communication tools to act as a mentor and a guide for your family in this process. Model compassionate listening and speaking. Your meditation practice will help you maintain focus and stability here.

Benefits of Win-Win

Win-win problem solving doesn't mean that we always get the solution we *want*, but it does ensure that everyone's *needs* are met. Children are much more likely to cooperate because their needs are getting met. Plus, they appreciate a seat at the decision-making table. Rather than the feeling of powerlessness they get from constant orders and demands from others, this method empowers children to speak up and consider others at the same time—a valuable skill in life!

When we think about the deeper messages behind this method of conflict resolution, we see that win-win helps us mentor children to work cooperatively with others in the future. It teaches them to consider others' needs, coaching them in empathy and perspective taking. Because win-win is a discussion, it teaches children to talk out their disagreements rather than use power. Imagine what the world would be like if every child grew up with these values!

Handling Sibling Conflicts

As you may know from your own experience (if you had a brother or sister), sibling conflicts are a normal part of life and will happen a *lot*. We should accept the reality of this. We should also not take on their problems as our own, so we'll be better able to weather the storms and help them get through it. These relationships have a powerful impact on our lives, but from the beginning it's not easy.

How do we help young children express their needs, stand up for themselves, and listen to their siblings? How do we help two, or even three, small children work through strong emotions at the same time? How do we create a family culture of cooperation and support so that sibling love can flourish?

Happily, there are proven ways to get our kids' relationships with each other off to a positive start and keep them on track for a good relationship going forward. We can give them skills to help them understand and express their own feelings while navigating their relationships with others. In *Peaceful Parent, Happy Siblings* (2015), Dr. Laura Markham shares three tenets of raising peaceful siblings: our own self-regulation, prioritizing connection, and aiming to "coach, not control."

Create a foundation of self-regulation. We can't completely control our children, but we can shift the patterns in our families by changing our own thoughts, words, and actions. Role modeling is the most powerful form of teaching. Our own self-regulation is the hardest work any of us do, and it is the most essential ingredient to raising peaceful siblings. This is where our mindfulness practices come into play: RAIN for handling our own difficult feelings, plus slow, deep breaths. Remember, the best way to regulate our feelings is with steady, daily meditation practice, which brings more calm and equanimity into our lives.

Parents who regulate their emotions have children who learn to manage their own feelings and therefore their own behavior—including toward their siblings. They can calm themselves more easily, so they fight less.

Prioritize your connection with each child. Instead of trying to figure out who's right and becoming the judge and jury over their conflicts, make maintaining a warm connection with each child your primary goal. Connection is what motivates children to follow our guidance. We can't really *make* anyone do something without using force. Our children have to *choose* to do what we say. Children who feel connected are more likely to cooperate with their parents and are more generous with their siblings.

Coach instead of controlling. Instead of force, a coach uses influence, teaching children to be their best. Controlling, on the other hand, is forcing a child to behave as you'd like by threatening punishment. Kids raised with punishment learn to use it against their siblings to increase their own standing and power. It gives them incentive to tattle on each other. When siblings are punished for fighting with each other, they become more resentful of each other and focused on revenge.

Think of yourself as their coach. In deciding when to step in, a coach gauges his or her players' skills and abilities. The coach may be more involved as children are learning and become more hands-off later. As siblings grow up and have more practice with handling their problems, you can step aside more and give them the valuable autonomous experience. Kids need to be able to make their own mistakes and learn from them. (If you're worried about safety, however, it's always a good idea to step in.)

How do we coach? The crucial first move is to pause. Take a moment to breathe deeply and center yourself so that you can respond thoughtfully instead of react. If you can do this part, the rest will come more easily!

What do we say when kids are fighting? Remember the skillful communication you've learned in previous chapters. Instead of throwing out orders, threats, judgments, and other communication barriers, acknowledge what is going on. Use I-messages and reflective listening. Acknowledging and describing what you see can take the situation down a notch.

Handling Sibling Conflicts: A Cheat Sheet

1. Pause, breathe, and center yourself. Say to yourself, *I'm helping my children.*

2. Say what you see. Acknowledge what is going on, describing without judgment.

3. Coach your children to express their feelings and articulate their needs.

4. Remember that you don't have to solve all their problems.

You may want to write these steps on sticky notes and place them strategically around your home.

As you help your children work through conflicts, invite them to get under the layer of solutions to the layer of needs. What does this look like in practice? Here are some examples:

Instead of: "Stop fighting! If you can't stop fighting, both of you are going to your rooms!"

Try: "I hear lots of yelling. You look really mad. I won't let you hit your brother. Can you tell him how you feel and what you are needing from him?"

Instead of: "No sticks! That's dangerous, give it to me!"

Try: "Whoa! I'm worried about that stick, and it looks like Taylor is too. She doesn't want the stick so close to her. You can swing it over there where it's away from your sister, or put it down."

Instead of: "I've told you three times to stop poking your brother! That's it, go to your room."

Try: "Ava, look at your brother's face… he doesn't like that poking. And I don't like the loud voices inside, it makes my muscles tight. I'm not going to let you hurt him. What are you needing right now?"

When You Have More Than One Upset Child

There aren't any easy answers when everyone needs you at once. The reality is that you won't be able to fix every problem or comfort every hurt. However, simply making the effort goes a long way to model empathy and concern for others with our children.

You *can* breathe, staying calm and grounded, through this moment. If you need to, take a moment to help yourself calm down. Here are some tactics for handling a complex situation.

When both need you at once, try to tend to them both. This isn't always easy, but it's often possible. Describe what is happening: "I have two upset children who are both hurting! Come here, there is plenty of room in my arms. You can cry as much as you want, then we'll sort this out and make things better."

If you need to go to one child over the other, speak to the child you aren't going to. This may be an instance when one child is hurt physically and needs tending right away even as the other is hurt emotionally: "Lucas, I hear that you are hurting and you need me, and I will be right there. I'm helping your brother with his knee, then I will help you with your feelings."

Take care of the feelings first. When emotions are running high, the learning centers in the brain shut down, so it's a bad time for solving problems—don't try to do that right away. Once the feelings have been expressed and acknowledged, and everyone is calming down, *then* coach your children to talk about what they are each needing in that moment.

Beginning Anew: A Tool for Bringing Closeness out of Conflict

No matter how skillful and grounded we are, there will still be conflicts and problems in our families. The tools of mindfulness meditation, loving-kindness, reflective listening, I-messages, and more will greatly reduce the number and severity of those conflicts, but we will still have them. Conflicts can, however, bring us even closer together if we use these moments as opportunities to be real and vulnerable, and to come together to repair the damage done.

On a retreat with Thich Nhat Hanh, I learned the Beginning Anew framework for repairing a relationship—including a relationship with a child. It teaches us to look deeply and honestly at ourselves and our past actions, speech, and thoughts. We take this moment as a fresh beginning for ourselves and in our relationships with others.

Beginning Anew has three parts: offering appreciation, sharing regrets, and expressing hurts and difficulties. You can do this in person, or write a letter of Beginning Anew if your child reads.

Part 1: Offering appreciation. This is an opportunity to shine light on the other's strengths and contributions, and to encourage the growth of his or her positive qualities. You may mention specific instances when the other person said or did something that you appreciated. This first step shows that you see the wonderful things about this person.

Part 2: Sharing regrets. This is your chance to mention any unskillful actions, speech, or thoughts that you feel bad about and haven't yet had an opportunity to apologize for. For example, you might say, "I'm sorry that I said you were selfish. I was wrong to do that. I realize how my comment hurt you, and I shouldn't have spoken in that way."

Part 3: Expressing hurts and difficulties. Now you share how you felt hurt by something the other person did or said. Use your I-messages here. Don't attack or blame. Speak or write about your hurts in a calm way, never in an exaggerated, reproachful, accusatory, or desperate manner. Speak or write from the heart, avoiding the communication barriers we covered in chapter 6.

Exercise: Write a Letter of Beginning Anew

Write and send a letter (or email) of Beginning Anew to someone you love. Then write about the experience in your *Raising Good Humans* journal. What was that person's reaction? Did it bring you closer?

Note: you can also use just the first two steps of Beginning Anew (appreciation and regrets) when you don't have a specific hurt or difficulty to discuss.

Beginning Anew gives us a framework to communicate skillfully instead of falling back into old, unskillful language. The goal is to repair the relationship. When we have a stronger relationship with our children, our influence grows in proportion.

You can use the process of Beginning Anew with many different relationships in your life. I've written letters of Beginning Anew to both of my parents, which helped us come together in a more authentic way. I've had a client use the process with her superior at work, and it helped her daily work life enormously! Consider this a powerful tool for all of your relationships.

The Power of Influence

As we start to shift away from using raw power over our children, our influence grows—a benefit we'll appreciate as our children get older. I believe that adolescent rebellion is not a reaction against parents themselves but against the unskillful or harsh discipline methods parents use. After years of inner resistance and resentment, as children gain more independence in their teen years, they naturally rebel against their parents' authoritarian ways. However, if we have limited our use of power and instead grown our *influence*, then our children will be more likely to trust and be open to our input. Our relationships will be stronger, closer, and more cooperative. All of this hinges on how we deal with the inevitable conflicts that arise throughout childhood.

When we work together to solve problems and recognize each person's needs, conflicts bring us closer together. Unresolved conflicts, festering over time, can be extremely toxic for a relationship. Children often nurture old wounds and skew parents' motives if the conflict is not discussed. When we are able to discuss what happened in a loving, nonjudgmental way, our children learn that they will be seen and heard, and that we take their needs seriously. Their trust in us grows and builds over time. They learn to listen to and empathize with our needs too.

It won't always work out. There will be times when you find yourself using power as a parent. There may even be times when that is the more skillful choice. However, the less you use power—and the more you approach problems in terms of meeting needs—the stronger your relationship will be and the more your influence will grow.

Our children need our influence in the turbulent teen years. As they are moving toward independence, when life feels uncertain, they need us to be on their side as guides and mentors. The tools in this chapter will help both you and your child solve problems skillfully without damaging the relationship, which will help you keep the lines of communication open for when your kid needs you most.

The foundation of this approach is in your *intention* to be present and curious—your intention to help your child. In those difficult moments, don't act right away. Pause, be present in the moment, and give yourself a chance at a skillful, compassionate response. What need is your child trying to meet? What are your needs?

Shifting to this point of view can be freeing. Using win-win problem solving, you don't have to be the judge and jury for your child. You don't need to have all the answers all the time. Instead, you can have a human-to-human relationship. You can get your own needs met *and* help your child get his needs met. In the next chapter, I'll share a few more tools to help support your peaceful home.

What to Practice This Week

- Sitting Meditation or body scan meditation for five to ten minutes, four to six days per week

- Loving-Kindness meditation four to six days per week

- Win-Win Problem Solving

- Write a letter of Beginning Anew

CHAPTER 8

Supporting Your Peaceful Home

"The greatest gifts you can give your children are the roots of responsibility and the wings of independence."

—Denis Waitley

Every day when my daughters get off the school bus, I try to be there. And by "be there" I mean be fully present, as best I can, letting go of my worries from the day, centering myself, and becoming calm in my body. I give them each a big hug, and I tell them, "I'm so happy to see you!" And I really am. I want each daughter to know that she really lights up my world, and that I am there for her. After they play for a while near the bus stop with our neighbors, we walk home together. I know that the strength of our relationship lies in these little moments and in the rhythms and rituals that shape each day.

As we've seen, mindful parenting is not about a technique to create an outcome but about building a loving *relationship* for life. Our connected relationships are the only way to cultivate willing cooperation. Children want to please us when they're treated with love, compassion, respect—and when their own stress levels aren't too high.

How do you cultivate that strong connection and maintain balance in their days? The skills you've learned so far—mindfulness meditation, disarming your triggers, loving-kindness, reflective listening, I-messages, and mindful problem solving—already constitute a road map to a strong relationship. In this chapter, I'll share with you other habits that will strengthen your connection with your child and support your peaceful home.

Consciously Cultivate Connection

The relationship we have with our children is the glue that holds us together. It's truly the very foundation of raising a good human. That is why all the work we've done with mindfulness and self-compassion comes foremost, to ground us—so we can connect and show that love. The more our children experience our unconditional love, the safer and more relaxed they feel. When they see the love in our eyes, they feel valued and value us back. They feel trust and trust us back.

All of this love creates a positive feedback loop, making parenting easier over time. We can create strong relationships not only by using the tools in the previous chapters but by intentionally spending our time and attention to cultivate a loving connection.

Connect with Physical Touch

Recently, my eight-year-old daughter was mad at me, and there was no one else around to offer her comfort. She was sobbing. When I went to her, she said, "Go away!" I stayed and sat behind her to gently rub her back. Even though her problem was with me, this affectionate touch soothed her and she eventually climbed into my lap. Snuggling helped her calm down and regulate her feelings.

Being touched and touching someone else are fundamental modes of human interaction. Positive physical touch is a powerful way to communicate affection, care, and concern for your child. Hugs, kisses, and cuddles reassure children of our presence, decrease their stress response, and help them regulate their own emotions.

How much loving touch should we offer? The "mother of family therapy," Virginia Satir, famously said, "We need four hugs a day for survival. We need eight hugs a day for maintenance. We need twelve hugs a day for growth." So indeed, as often as possible. Make lots of hugs and snuggles a habit when your child is younger, and he may still want to stay close as he ages. Although it's rare that I get to hold hands now with my eleven-year-old, she'll often lean into me for that close, physical affection.

Cuddles and hugs are vital and essential forms of physical touch that children thrive on, but did you know that roughhousing and wrestling are great for kids too? Laurence Cohen, psychologist and play expert, tells us that aggressive, physical play can help children express their feelings, learn impulse control, and build confidence.

How do you roughhouse? He provides a simple explanation for parents in his book, *Playful Parenting* (2001, p. 101): "You say, 'Let's wrestle!' She says, 'What's that?' You say, 'You try to pin me down using all your strength you try to get me on my back with both my shoulders on the floor (or, you try to get past me onto the couch, but you can't sneak around, you have to use all your strength to go right past me)."

Roughhousing helps children physically connect with us in an active way, burning off some of their energy. It builds children's physical strength and creativity, and connects us to them physically and emotionally. Just remember these rules about roughhousing: pay attention, let your child win (most of the time), and always stop if someone is hurt. Just as with tickling, when a child says stop, stop right away. This teaches our children that their body deserves respect and that they are in charge of their own body.

Whether it's wrestling, cuddling, or hugs, intentionally connect with your child physically. Touch is soothing and helps children regulate their emotions. It's a great way to keep your relationship strong.

Connect with Play

Many of us busy adults (me included!) have resistance to getting down on the floor and playing with our children. Can't they just play on their own? The very idea of Candy Land makes me want to run and hide. Yes, children can and should have independent play time, but we should take time to enter into their world too. Play is the currency of childhood. Children need play like they need air and water. It helps them understand the world, heal hurts, and develop confidence in their abilities. When we connect with our children playfully, we refill their cups with love, encouragement, and enthusiasm. Moreover, it helps us literally and figuratively "loosen up," which we might need!

Saying yes to play with your child doesn't have to be onerous or take up a lot of time. In fact, kids are often ready to move on after just a short while. Set a timer for ten minutes and dive in whole-heartedly for that time. Think of it as a "playing meditation," and practice being fully present, noticing when your mind wanders and judges. Practice paying attention to your child with kindness and curiosity. Play gives you a wonderful opportunity to find out who your child is today—to discover this human being anew.

Don't remember how to play? Just follow your child's lead—temporarily give her the power she craves in a world in which she is mostly powerless. Often your role will be minimal. You might be the audience for a skit or a dance. You might just wave goodbye and cry mock dramatic tears as your child leaves for the moon. You can also play by being silly and getting your child to giggle. Pretending to bumble or fall down is hilarious to a child. You can give your child "Special Time," as described below.

Whatever form your play takes, practice being fully present. Practice appreciating this time, knowing that it is fleeting as your child grows and becomes more independent.

Practice: "Special Time"

Special Time is a way for us to give kids what they crave: 100 percent of our attention without any distractions. The premise is that you let your child lead the way (while keeping him safe), and you agree to be up for anything. Parents who try this exercise often see significant positive changes in their child's behavior. Why? Because it shores up that essential connection.

Here's how to do it:

1. **Announce Special Time.** Say to your child, "I'll play whatever you want to play for ten minutes. The only things we can't do are read or use screens. What do you want to play?"

2. **Set a timer.** Ten minutes is great, but five minutes will do. After a while, try twenty minutes and see how that feels. Special Time needs boundaries around it to signal that the rules aren't the same as in regular life.

3. **Let your child lead.** During this time, put your squeamishness, your preferences, your worries, and your judgment aside, and let your child try the thing you wouldn't choose to do in a million years. If he wants you to pull him back and forth on an old skateboard until he falls over, over, and over, resist "teach-

ing" him how to skate, consider it your workout for the day, and make it fun.

4. **Resist the urge to judge or evaluate your child.** *Don't take control or suggest your own ideas unless your child asks.*

5. **Refrain from checking your phone.** *Just show up and give your child the gift of being seen and acknowledged. As best you can, be fully present.*

6. **End Special Time when the timer sounds.** *If your child has a tantrum or is upset, offer him the same empathetic listening you would for any upset feelings.*

Special Time is a way to put those essential deposits in your relationship bank account. Some parents offer Special Time daily or several times a week. Try this out and see how your child responds.

Connect by Working Together

Children want to be able to do all the things that adults do. Encourage this! Children can and should work with us in daily life. It might start with having a sturdy stool in the kitchen so that our children can help wash the potatoes and peel carrots. Very young children can wipe up spills, set out the napkins, help feed the cat, and so on. As they grow, their responsibilities should grow too. When children contribute to the smooth running of the house, it fosters their sense of capability, which is empowering. Think of your child as part of your family "team."

In fact, research has shown that a child who does chores has a greater chance of success later in life! Dr. Marilynn Rossman, professor of family education at University of Minnesota, looked at data from longitudinal studies to look at "success" defined as not using drugs, having quality relationships, finishing education, and getting started in a career. She concluded that the most successful kids *started doing chores at three to four years of age*, whereas those who waited until their teen years to start doing chores were less successful. Psychiatrist Edward Hallowell says that chores create a kind of "can-do, want-to-do feeling" that fosters young adults with a feeling of capability (Lythcott-Haimes 2015).

A lifetime of capability and responsibility starts with you taking the time to connect through working together. Expect (and insist) that your young one does his part, knowing that when you are teaching him how to do the laundry and make the bed, you are teaching him life skills.

Connect with Verbal Encouragement

Positive words of encouragement let our children know that we believe in them and that we're in their corner. Instead of growing into adults with Mom or Dad's critical voice in their heads, our children can use words of support and confidence to motivate themselves and reinforce positive behaviors.

Rather than "Good job," use I-messages to praise your child honestly and descriptively. Instead of vague, general words, be specific in your encouragement: "When you gave that bike a try even though it was scary, I really appreciated your courage." Here are a few other phrases that can create connection through encouragement:

Thank you for your kindness.

I really appreciate how hard you tried for that.

What you did was very generous.

You showed enormous strength in handling this challenge.

I love your sense of skepticism!

Your imagination is awesome!

Thank you for reminding me how fun it is to be playful.

A warm, positive connection is the fuel for a cooperative relationship with your child. When you intentionally, consciously connect, you put deposits in your relationship bank account—allowing for inevitable withdrawals later. Positive physical touch, play, working together, and praise are just a few of the many ways you can connect. Make it a point to ensure that your child knows you see her, hear her, and love her often. This will fortify your relationship through the inevitable rough times that life brings.

Effective Parenting Habits

Kids need unconditional love, mentorship, and healthy boundaries. When we've focused on mindfulness, skillful communication, and positive connection, setting limits becomes easier, but it's not always a walk in the park. Habits of responsibility, consistency, and fostering independence will help make parenting easier.

Responsibilities Before Fun

Setting healthy boundaries means tempering our children's wild nature (but not crushing it) and mentoring our children in how to be (ultimately) good adults. Sometimes in our efforts to avoid old-school threats-and-punishment methods, we swing too far in the other direction and fail to set firm-enough limits. When kids push at boundaries, our job is to gently and insistently hold them firm so we don't end up with children who run roughshod over others' needs.

It helps enormously to save the fun stuff for *after* they've taken care of their responsibilities. In my home, this means that screen time comes after my girls put away their backpacks, feed the cats, empty the dishwasher, and set the table. It could be that dessert happens after your child clears and wipes the table. Whatever it is for you, your parenting life will be easier if you establish a culture of responsibilities before privileges.

Please don't use this approach as a threat, as in: "If you don't do _____, you won't get _____." Instead, think of it as, "*First* we do _____ [responsibility], *then* we do _____ [fun thing]."

When you establish in your home a culture of responsibilities, then it's not a threat to lose the privilege, it's simply a natural consequence. When your child inevitably misses a fun thing because he didn't take care of a chore, practice remaining calm and nonreactive, because this is not your problem. Instead, respond empathetically to their feelings, but hold your boundary lovingly.

Consistency and Rhythm

Life with children becomes much easier when we have a fairly consistent pattern to our days and weeks. Because so much of our children's lives is beyond their control, it helps them enormously to be able to orient themselves within a stable rhythm. If they know what to expect from their days, they are much less likely to resist at each step.

Daily Rhythm

Bring regularity to your child's days by starting the night before with a consistent, early bedtime. Children need a *lot* of sleep. A lack of sufficient sleep makes children cranky, prone to tantrums, uncooperative, and more likely to get sick. Poor sleep also impairs their growth.

How do you know if your child is getting enough sleep? Answer: When your child wakes up on her own, without an alarm, feeling refreshed.

If your child is a toddler, hold on to that naptime for as long as possible. Even when your child graduates from a midday nap, it's helpful for your child (and you!) to have a quiet, restful, solitary time during the day to restore her spirits and act as a pressure valve for the day. She can have quiet time in her room even if she is not sleeping.

When I was home with my preschool-age children, I took them to the YMCA almost every day. I had my midmorning workout, and they went to childcare. This habit met my needs for exercise and time out of the house, and their needs for routine and socialization, in one fell swoop. It became an anchoring force in my day as a stay-at-home-mom.

What do you do regularly? You may have work, school, childcare, and other factors that create a routine in your day. Embrace that structure and it will make your life with kids easier. If you don't have a steady rhythm, use the exercise below to help you establish one.

Exercise: Create a Consistent Daily Rhythm

In addition to a consistent sleep and waking time, kids thrive on routine throughout their day. Here's how to schedule some daily consistency.

1. Make a List of All of Your Daily Tasks

Gather information on what you need to get done daily. Don't worry about how you organize this list; this is a brain dump, not a to-do list. Take a few minutes to jot down everything you do each day (and everything you miss but should be doing) in your *Raising Good Humans* journal. Better yet, capture all of the tasks you need to get done in a day on your smartphone.

If you already have a routine...
Divide the tasks into the following:

- Tasks you already do that work well for you

- Tasks you need to add into your routine

If you're starting from scratch...
Begin by answering these questions:

- What tasks do you need to complete each day in order to get out the door?

- Which tasks do you need to do each day to care for your child?

- Which tasks do you need to do each day to eat?

- Which errands do you need to get done daily?

- When do you want to fit in a short meditation practice?

- Which tasks need to get done in order for you to get some exercise?

- Which tasks do you need to get done to maintain an organized home?

Make the list. In the beginning, no task is too small. If you want to work "brush teeth" into your routine, that's great. Throw everything in and edit later.

2. Create a Schedule

Now assess your energy levels. Think about when you do your best work. Most people have greater energy in the morning. It's important to schedule in the things that require the most energy from you. Think about the schedule as a rhythm, a guide to structure your days rather than a rigid routine. In your journal, write the tasks that are best handled at:

- Morning

- Midday

- Evening

3. Create a New Daily Rhythm, Adding in Some Flexibility

In setting a rhythm, try to harness your most productive time of day for your most challenging tasks, and your least productive time to do the more mundane tasks. Match up your activities with points during the day, starting with anything that has to be done at a certain time (like picking up your kids from school or eating lunch). Then slot in tasks based on when you think it makes the most sense to tackle them.

4. Test-Drive Your New Routine

Take your new routine for a test-drive for a few weeks. How does it feel? Did you schedule your tasks and activities at times that make sense? Do you need to make some tweaks? Adjust anything that is not working as needed. Assess your daily rhythm, and see how your new routine is working for you.

Weekly Rhythm

You can also give your week a sense of order, consistency, and flow by creating rhythms that support your family. In our home, the week is book-marked by "Screen-free Sunday." Even if you are not religious, it's a great idea to have a weekly sabbath day—a day of rest that might include time in nature or connecting with family.

In our family, we adopted this wonderful idea from *Simplicity Parenting* by Kim Payne: a predictable rhythm for dinners. In our house it is vegetarian on Sunday, pizza on Monday, pasta on Tuesday, soup on Wednesday, rice on Thursday, fish on Friday, and Saturday is open. Keeping to this rhythm helped my young children know what day of the week it was and made them less resistant about meals. It also made stepping out of the rhythm with a night at a restaurant a real treat.

Weekly rhythms can be created from a school schedule, classes, or responsibilities that you can involve your children in such as laundry or cleaning, or even regular hikes or downtime. What happens in your home every week? How can you make the week more rhythmic?

Help Children Develop Independence

When I was in graduate school, I learned about the Montessori system of education. Maria Montessori, the groundbreaking educator, realized that when adults facilitate the proper environment, we can tap into children's *intrinsic* desire to learn and be independent. Today, we can walk into a Montessori classroom and see children as young as two purposely "working"— often utterly absorbed in their tasks. Why are they so independently industrious? For starters, everything is at their level. There are shorter chairs, sinks, hooks, and even brooms and mops! The environment is simple and tidy, with space to move around and a place for everything. And children are given some power. They are allowed to choose their work from a prescribed range of options.

What can we take from this method to apply at home? When my daughter started going to a Montessori classroom at the age of two and learned how to scramble eggs, I realized that she was much more capable than I was giving her credit for. Children can and want to do more even at young ages. At home, we can modify our environment to give them more power and independence.

Imagine that you are three feet tall and trying to get around your home. Could you get yourself a glass of water? Can you reach the paper towels to clean up? Can you hang up your own jacket? Most likely no. When you are a little person in a big person's world, it's often impossible to do anything by yourself. Go through your home and make simple modifications to foster your child's desire to "do it myself":

- Install hooks at the right level for your child to hang a coat.

- Put a small stainless-steel pitcher and sturdy cups where he can reach them for pouring water.

- Make sure sponges and rags are within his reach for cleanup.

- Have a sturdy kitchen stool that your child can move around on his own.

As much as you can, give your young one actual tools to use. In the Recommended Reading and Resources section in this book, I've shared the

For Small Hands website catalog, which offers real tools—rakes, brooms, and more—that are child-size. When my daughters were little, they used a wavy stainless-steel cutter that they could hold with both hands to help me chop vegetables. They also had a spray bottle (with an all-natural white vinegar and water solution) to help spray and clean the windows and tables.

When you modify your environment to help your child be independent early, you set up healthy expectations of capability and contribution. You don't have to be the servant, jumping up to fetch your child a glass of water. Let him do it himself, and you will develop a more self-reliant, competent kid. It takes more time at first to facilitate your child's helping, but by doing some work upfront, things become easier over the long term. It's an investment that pays off.

Simplify to Support Your Peaceful Home

One of the biggest challenges to parenting mindfully is the problem of *too much*. We all seem to struggle with stress from packed schedules and an over-abundance of stuff. Yet like the proverbial frog in the pot of water that slowly heats to boiling, we often don't recognize the problem until it is overwhelming. Our commercial culture screams at us to go, go, go and buy, buy, buy as the way to happiness, but just as too many sweets will make us sick, too much stuff and a packed schedule leave us stressed, anxious, and unable to appreciate the abundance that we have.

Children, who are less acclimated to our busy lifestyles, feel the stress and react in ways that can be unpredictable. On their own, children naturally move at a much slower pace (as you have probably noticed), living fully in the moment and exploring their worlds deeply. Too much activity deprives children of the time to see, touch, smell, and listen to the world. It deprives them of the space to explore and get to know themselves.

I invite you to join me in pushing back against our "more is better culture" for the sake of your child (and your own sanity). Instead, let's simplify and foster our children's natural sense of safety, peacefulness, and wonder.

Simplify Schedules

A friend of mine told me the story of a family with adolescent children who were suffering from anxiety and going to therapy. They would arrive at their session squeezed in between gymnastics and soccer, eating fast food on the way over because there was no time for dinner. Every day was packed with activities and events that, taken individually, are wonderful, but added together created a schedule with zero downtime. It didn't take much to see that the children's anxiety was perpetuated, if not triggered, by their overly full days.

As children's schedules have become increasingly full, their mental health has collectively taken a downward slide. Colleges and universities have begun to notice the impact on their students. A 2013 American College Health Association survey of almost one hundred thousand students found that more than half of students felt overwhelmed, very sad, and overwhelming anxiety (Lythcott-Haims 2015). While the intent is good, loading kids' schedules with extracurricular "enrichment" activities actually has an adverse effect on them.

Children (heck, all of us) need free time to balance out their activities, get to know themselves, and feel peaceful. Imagine children who are absorbed deeply in pretend play. They are completely focused, and the world around them disappears. This is one of the most vital activities children can do— processing their world and their feelings, healing hurts, and expanding their creativity in their own time and at their own pace. Without it, children tend to be more nervous and less able to relax or sleep (Payne 2009).

We can't instigate this state, we can't take classes to "enrich" this kind of creativity. Instead, we can only leave time and space for unsupervised (but safe) free play and trust that downtime is essential to our children's creativity and evolving identity. A rushed schedule packed full of activities does not allow for this; instead it promotes stress.

You may be worried that your child will be bored if you allow time for free, unstructured play. You're right. However, it's good for children to feel bored! In *Simplicity Parenting*, author and counselor-therapist Kim Payne characterizes boredom as a "gift," describing it as the precursor to creativity. In my own experience, I've found this to be true again and again. When my daughters were little, we gave them a lot of unstructured time for play, from which grew a bounty of skits, forts, drawings, puppets, and elaborate worlds for their stuffed animals.

What do we say when our children complain of being bored? I recommend Payne's single, flatline response: "Something to do is right around the corner." Don't rescue them and don't entertain them. They'll find something to do.

When all of your friends are signing up their preschoolers for soccer and tumbling, you might worry that simplifying your schedule to allow time for free play will put your kids at a disadvantage. Don't. Time for children's play without guidance and purpose is no less than developmentally *vital*.

From more than six thousand "play histories" of patients, psychiatrist and researcher Stuart Brown has found a direct correlation between play behavior and happiness, from childhood into adulthood. Children deprived of play have difficulty regulating appropriate emotions and exhibit a lack of resilience and curiosity. These children are often rigid and aggressive (Brown 2009). Dr. Brown studied murderers in Texas prisons and found that *none* of the men had ever experienced normal rough-and-tumble play, not even one. These violent, antisocial men missed the learning that came from play. Unstructured play teaches children to moderate their behavior and helps children develop self-control—essential parts of being human.

Our diminishing leisure time is detrimental for children. We must fight back and take back our time. Do you have your child in multiple groups or activities? Do you hurry from one thing to the next? Take steps to simplify your schedule and protect your child's time. You don't have to say yes to every birthday party or event in your circle of friends. There's so much happening in our lives today that our job is often to curate events instead of seeking them out. Ideally, give your child unstructured free time *every day* to play and daydream. When you have a busy day, balance that with a calm day. When you simplify your child's schedule, you'll be giving her the lifelong gift of a true childhood.

Simplify the Environment

Our lives are full—not only of events but of stuff. Right from the time a woman is expecting, our culture bombards her with a never-ending list of "required" purchases. Later, children's rooms become overflowing with toys, drawers jam-packed, walls covered in posters, closets packed tight, and floors hidden beneath a multicolored, ever-expanding layer of *stuff*. In *Simplicity Parenting*, Kim Payne suggests that this profusion of products and playthings is not just a symptom of excess but a *cause* of stress, fragmentation, and overload in children. He argues that our consumer culture creates a sense of entitlement in children. It also creates a false reliance on purchases rather than on people to satisfy and sustain us emotionally (Payne 2009).

Imagine a huge pile of toys. Our children find it overwhelming because there are too many choices. They don't know what's in the middle of the pile, and they don't value any of it very highly. When faced with an excess of choices, children learn to undervalue their playthings and choose to hold out for something more. Moreover, cleanup becomes an overwhelming trial. While we want to be generous, provide well, and stimulate their imaginations, the result for our children too often is a sense of overload from too much stuff.

When my daughter was two years old, I realized that the growing piles of stuff were starting to overwhelm our home. I was a little worried about throwing things away, but I took steps to simplify her environment nonetheless. While she was at preschool, I radically decluttered her room, taking the majority of toys away and leaving a spacious, appealing space. When she returned home, I was nervous about her reaction. Would she freak out and have a tantrum, demanding her stuff back? To my surprise, she was delighted with her room. She thanked me for making it so beautiful and immediately began to play.

Children feel a sense of ease and focus in a room with less. It's soothing to the senses and can even help to calm behavioral issues. Simplifying means less clutter and more breathing room. Children appreciate their things more. Fewer belongings means reducing the burden of our responsibilities. We spend less time on care, maintenance, searching for items, and storage. Less stuff actually means more ease. It means more time to devote to what is really important.

How to simplify? I suggest starting with toys. Pick a time when your child is not at home. Then gather up and radically reduce the number of toys. Some you can discard completely, some you may want to cycle in and out of your kid's space. Be careful though! Try putting things in a basement or storage area for a few weeks, that way you can retrieve a particularly beloved toy. Kim Payne suggests a list of toys for the discard pile, including:

Broken toys

Developmentally inappropriate toys—too old or too young for your child

Character toys from movies

Toys that "do too much" and break too easily

Very high-stimulation toys

Annoying or offensive toys

Toys you were pressured to buy

Toy multiples

What's left? Keep toys that encourage pretend play and creativity, such as real tools, dolls and puppets, musical instruments, and so forth. I remember thinking that those crunchy mamas were crazy giving their children scarves to play with, but it turns out that they are a wonderful toy! Scarves can become all manner of dress-up items, structural supports, theater curtains, and more.

Keep things that your child can project any number of different imaginative ideas upon. Have out only what your child can put away by herself in five minutes, arranged in a pleasing fashion. Also rotate items in and out, which makes things feel like new again.

Once you simplify the toys, cast an eye to the other areas of your child's life and home. You might be able to reduce the number of clothes in your child's drawers to make getting ready easier in the morning. You might reduce the excess in the rest of your home for more ease and freedom. Remember, we are always modeling for our children. Less stuff means less to take care of and more time to focus on what's important.

Simplify Screens

Our children are growing up in a vastly different world than we did. Now we walk around with a portal to every kind of information and entertainment burning a hole in our pockets. Screens are as mesmerizing and irresistible to children as they are to us, so if we want them to grow up grounded in reality, it behooves us to set limits on screen time.

I invite you to consider the issue of kids and screen time from the stance of the middle path. Neither of the extremes—unlimited access or a complete ban—teach children how to live mindfully in a world where screens are ubiquitous. Digital technology offers great opportunities for creativity, problem solving, and learning. My daughter was thrilled when she learned how to code a game, and I was pleased to see it. Yet, the digital world also has content that's oversexualized and violent, and the time spent on screens takes time away from interacting in the real world. The American College of Pediatricians (2016) warns that too much screen time can lead to obesity, sleep problems, depression, and anxiety. Clearly, digital technology has a big impact on our lives, so the question is how to set healthy limits on it.

Look at your own relationship to technology. Do you like to watch TV or play games online? Are you constantly checking your phone? Do you talk on the phone when you're driving? Do you put limits around your screen time? Kids see how we live and learn from that. When you ask yourself, *What is healthy for my child?* look to see what shifts you can make in your own technology use first. Think of yourself as your child's media model, teaching her how to live a balanced life with digital technology.

What kinds of limits are good for kids? It's ideal to hold off on screen time all together when they're babies. Once your child is older than two, you may wish to introduce some content. But be choosy about the quality of what you're giving your child, and limit the amount of time. When she is older, talk to your child about how you feel about screen time. You can use win-win problem solving to set healthy limits together. Throughout childhood, think of screen time as an evolving conversation to which you can apply a sense of mindful curiosity.

Screen time tips:

- Use password protection on devices so that your child must ask you to unlock them.

- Set parental controls on devices to filter and block violence and pornography.

- Establish time limits for screen time.

- Keep all screens and technology out in "public" family spaces. Charge your phones in public/family spaces.

- Don't give your child screen time thirty minutes to an hour before bedtime. The bright light can interrupt your child's sleep.

- Resist handing your child your phone while waiting in line or driving in the car if you can.

- Have a weekly digital detox day (or part of the day). We have "screen-free Sunday" in our home.

- Make sure responsibilities such as chores and homework are done before screen time.

- No one has phones at the dinner table.

- Insist on some fresh air and exercise before screen time.

- Delay giving your child a smartphone. Consider doing the "Wait Until Eighth" pledge to empower parents to resist the pressure to get a smartphone earlier.

Instead of turning on a screen, your child can play with toys, draw, read books, or help out with chores around the house. Audio books and podcasts for kids are great alternatives to screen time. And remember that it's okay (even good) for your child to be bored sometimes. However, *you must walk the talk*. I used to keep my phone in my room to use as an alarm clock until my daughter called me out on it. We weren't supposed to have technology in our rooms. So I moved it downstairs and bought myself an alarm clock. Model the kind of media use you want for your child. With healthy limits, we show our kids how to maintain a balanced relationship with our digital technology.

The environment in your home has a big impact on your ability to stay grounded and communicate skillfully with your child. Rather than being overwhelmed by clutter and busyness, you can choose to move toward a slower pace and more simplicity in your life. When you reduce stress and distraction, it becomes easier to practice meditation and bring mindfulness and compassion into the rest of your life. It becomes easier to remember to connect lovingly with your child.

Shifting Toward a More Mindful Life

There's no one single thing that will turn your relationship with your child into a cooperative one. Instead, think of the tools and practices you've learned here as a guide for shifting bit by bit, over time. Changing things doesn't solely depend on how calm you are, what you say, or the relative clutter in your life, but all of these things do have an impact. It all starts with the one thing you have control over: you.

It's possible to take your frustrations in parenting and treat them as your teachers. Let the mistakes and missteps motivate you. When I think back to how I struggled as a young parent—to the times of sobbing on the floor in frustration, certain that I was failing—compared to where I am now, with positive, loving, (imperfect) human-to-human relationships with my children, I wouldn't change a thing. Those challenges showed me the learning I needed to do. The challenges were motivation to acquire the practical skills that I've shared with you here and to turn my family life around.

As you follow this path, please remember that there is no such thing as perfect. Accepting and expecting our inevitable human lapses help us to recognize our common humanity—for ourselves and our children. Don't beat yourself up when you yell. I still yell from time to time! Instead, consider it an opportunity to practice Beginning Anew—an opportunity to model for your child what to do when you mess up. As you follow this path, think *progress* not perfection.

On a Mindful Mama podcast, I asked a group of experts each the same question: "What do children need?" Prominent among the answers was *unconditional* love—loving our children whether they're having a good day or they're struggling. If children can grow up knowing unconditional love, it creates the best possible foundation for emotionally healthy adulthoods. A foundation that allows them to face all of life's challenges with strong roots. How do we give unconditional love? By leading with loving and accepting ourselves. Training regularly with meditation and loving-kindness practices can get you there. Keep at it.

Remember that our old habits are familiar and strong. It takes diligent practice to bring mindfulness into daily life and learn to respond to our children empathetically and skillfully. It might take a while, but don't give up! Be persistent in learning and practicing this new language. As your child grows, parenting will become easier and easier for you (just as it's getting harder and harder for your peers using the old modalities). Creating strong, lifelong relationships means keeping the long view in mind.

Your effort in raising good humans will positively impact not just your own family but also your community and generations to come. Children who grow up feeling seen, heard, and loved will be a powerful force for good. Children who know how to solve problems in ways that meet everyone's needs can help evolve the way we interact as humans. Your efforts will have ripple effects. But underneath all of that, you will have a loving relationship for life. Your effort here can make all the difference in the world to the person who means the most to you: your child.

What to Practice This Week and Beyond

- Sitting Meditation or body scan meditation for five to ten minutes
- Loving-Kindness practice
- Special Time
- Create a daily rhythm
- Simplify an area of your home

Acknowledgments

Writing can feel solitary, but the truth is that there's a village of people who helped me write this book. First, I want to thank my husband, Bill, who has been my first editor and unflagging supporter throughout this process. Thank you for believing in me.

To my family: Mom, thank you for your encouragement and kindness. Thank you for modeling open-minded curiosity and compassion. Jared, thank you for making me laugh—I love you so much. Sending a big dose of gratitude to my dad: may the temper that we share be a catalyst for good in the world. Thank you for your enthusiastic encouragement when I was a kid and always believing in me.

To Carla Naumburg: thank you for being such a great friend and champion of my work. I couldn't have done this without you. Your generosity and wisdom have made a huge difference in my life.

To my Mindful Parenting students: thank you for your honest sharing, for being real, and for taking this work into your lives.

To my editors: thank you for challenging me to grow my writing.

I can't leave this page without expressing my gratitude to my friends. Thank you for your hugs, your warmth, your wise advice, your listening, and more: Margaret Winslow, Jeannie Stith-Mawhinney, Sarah Andrus, Kari Gormley, Allana Taranto, Kate Castro, Jennifer Curley, Clare Consavage, Lindsey Mix, Lisa Surbrook, Andrea Zatarain, Annie Gutsche, Ariel Gruswitz, Judy Morris, Heather Toupin, Amanda Bostick, Kyara Beck, Meagan Bergeron, and Josie Marsh.

Finally, a deep bow of gratitude to my teachers: Thich Nhat Hanh, Tara Brach, Cathy and Todd Adams, Jack Kornfield, Dan Siegel and Mary Hartzell, and others. Without your wisdom and guidance, this book would not exist. Thank you for sharing your voice and helping to spark inspiration in me.

Recommended Reading and Resources

Books

Anh's Anger by Gail Silver

The Awakened Family by Shefali Tsabari

The Happiness Trap (illustrated) by Russ Harris

How to Be a Happier Parent by KJ Dell'Antonia

How to Stop Losing Your Sh*t with Your Kids by Carla Naumburg

How to Talk so Little Kids Will Listen by Joanna Faber and Julie King

Parent Effectiveness Training by Thomas Gordon

Parenting from the Inside Out by Daniel J. Siegel and Mary Hartzell

Peace of Mind: Becoming Fully Present by Thich Nhat Hanh

Planting Seeds: Practicing Mindfulness with Children by Thich Nhat Hanh

Playful Parenting by Lawrence J. Cohen

Real Happiness by Sharon Salzberg

Simplicity Parenting by Kim John Payne

Resources

For Small Hands catalog, https://forsmallhands.com

Go Zen online programs for children, https://gozen.com

Insight Timer app, https://insighttimer.com

Time-In Toolkit from Generation Mindful, https://genmindful.com

References

Adams, Cathy. 2014. *Living What You Want Your Kids To Learn*. Be U, an imprint of Wyatt-MacKenzie.

American College of Pediatricians. 2016. "The Impact of Media Use and Screen Time on Children, Adolescents, and Families." https://www .acpeds.org/the-college-speaks/position-statements/parenting-issues /the-impact-of-media-use-and-screen-time-on-children-adolescents-and -families

Bertelli, Cedric. "Turn on Your Healing Superpower with Cedric Bertelli," September 18, 2018, in *Mindful Mama*, produced by Hunter Clarke-Fields, Mindful Mama Mentor, 48:24, https://www.mindfulmamamen tor.com/blog/turn-on-your-healing-superpower-cedric-bertolli-133/.

Bögels, Susan, and Kathleen Restifo. 2014. *Mindful Parenting: A Guide for Mental Health Practitioners*. New York: Springer.

Brach, Tara. 2003. *Radical Acceptance*. New York, NY: Bantam Dell.

Brown, Brené. 2012. *Daring Greatly*. New York: Avery, an imprint of Penguin Random House.

Brown, Stuart. 2009. "Discovering the Importance of Play Through Personal Histories and Brain Images." *American Journal of Play* 1(4).

Cohen, Lawrence J. 2001. *Playful Parenting*. New York: Ballantine Books.

Corliss, Julie. 2014. "Mindfulness Meditation May Ease Anxiety, Mental Stress." *Harvard Health Blog*. Boston: Harvard Health Publishing.

Cullen, Margaret, and Gonzalo Brito Pons. 2016. "Taming the Raging Fire Within." *Mindful* 3(6): 56–63.

Davidson, Richard J., Jon Kabat-Zinn, Jessica Schumacher, Melissa Rosenkranz, Daniel Muller, Saki F. Santorelli, Ferris Urbanowski, Anne Harrington, Katherine Bonus, and John F. Sheridan. 2002. "Alterations in Brain and Immune Function Produced by Mindfulness Meditation." *Psychosomatic Medicine* 65(4): 564–570.

Dyer, Wayne W. 2004. *The Power of Intention*. CA: Hay House, Inc.

Fredrickson, B. L., M. A. Cohn, K. A. Coffey, J. Pek, and S. M. Finkel. 2008. "Open Hearts Build Lives: Positive Emotions, Induced Through Loving-Kindness Meditation, Build Consequential Personal Resources." *Journal of Personality and Social Psychology* 95(5): 1,045–1,062.

Gershoff, Elizabeth T., Andrew Grogan-Kaylor, Jennifer E. Lansford, Lei Chang, Arnaldo Zelli Kirby Deater-Deckard, and Kenneth A. Dodge. 2010. "Parent Discipline Practices in an International Sample: Associations with Child Behaviors and Moderation by Perceived Normativeness." *Child Development* 81(2): 487–502.

Gordon, Thomas. 1970. *Parent Effectiveness Training.* New York: David McKay Company, a division of Random House, Inc.

Ireland, Tom. 2014. "What Does Mindfulness Meditation Do to Your Brain?" *Scientific American Blog.* June 12. https://blogs.scientificamerican.com /guest-blog/what-does-mindfulness-meditation-do-to-your-brain

Kabat-Zinn, Jon. 1994. *Wherever You Go, There You Are.* New York: Hyperion.

Kabat-Zinn, Jon. 2013. *Full Catastrophe Living.* New York: Bantam Books.

Kabat-Zinn, Jon. 2018. *Meditation Is Not What You Think.* New York: Hyperion.

Lewis, Katherine Reynolds. 2018. *The Good News About Bad Behavior.* New York: Public Affairs.

Lythcott-Haims, Julie. 2015. *How to Raise an Adult.* New York: Henry Holt and Company, LLC.

Markham, Laura. 2015. *Peaceful Parent, Happy Siblings.* New York: Penguin Group.

McCraith, Sheila. 2014. *Yell Less Love More.* Boston: Fair Winds Press.

Neff, Kristin. 2011a. "The Motivational Power of Self-Compassion." *Huffington Post* July 29. https://www.huffpost.com/entry/self-compas sion_n_865912

Neff, Kristin. 2011b. *Self-Compassion.* New York: William Morrow, an imprint of HarperCollins Publishers.

Nhat Hanh, Thich. 2003. *No Death, No Fear.* New York: Riverhead Books.

Nhat Hanh, Thich. 1975. *The Miracle of Mindfulness.* Boston: Beacon Press.

Payne, Kim John. 2009. *Simplicity Parenting.* New York: Ballantine Books.

Salzberg, Sharon. 2011. *Real Happiness.* New York: Workman Publishing Company.

Seltzer, Leon F. 2016. "You Only Get More of What You Resist—Why?" *Psychology Today.* June 15. https://www.psychologytoday.com/us/blog /evolution-the-self/201606/you-only-get-more-what-you-resist-why

Shapiro, Shauna, and Chris White. 2014. *Mindful Discipline.* Oakland, CA: New Harbinger Publications.

Siegel, Daniel J. 2018. "The Science of Wellbeing—Dr. Dan Siegel." *Mindful Mama* podcast. October 30. https://www.mindfulmamamentor.com /blog/the-science-of-presence-dr-dan-siegel-139/

Siegel, Daniel J., and Mary Hartzell. 2014. *Parenting from the Inside Out*. New York: Jeremy P. Tarcher/Penguin, a member of Penguin Group.

Siegel, Daniel J., and Tina Payne Bryson. 2011. *The Whole-Brain Child*. New York: Bantam Books.

Sofer, Oren Jay. 2018. *Say What You Mean*. Boulder, CO: Shambala Publications, Inc.

Wang, Ming-Te and Sarah Kenny. 2013. "Longitudinal Links Between Fathers' and Mothers' Harsh Verbal Discipline and Adolescents' Conduct Problems and Depressive Symptoms." *Child Development* 85, (3): 908–923. https://doi.org/10.1111/cdev.12143

Winnicott, D. W. 1973. *The Child, the Family, and the Outside World*. London: Penguin Books.

Wiseman, Theresa. 1996. "A Concept Analysis of Empathy." *Journal of Advanced Nursing* 23(6): 1,162–1,167.

Hunter Clarke-Fields, MSAE, is a mindfulness mentor, coach, host of the *Mindful Mama* podcast, and creator of the Mindful Parenting online course. She coaches moms on how to cultivate mindfulness in their daily lives. Hunter has more than twenty years of experience in meditation and yoga practices, and has taught mindfulness to thousands worldwide.

Foreword writer **Carla Naumburg, PhD**, is a clinical social worker, writer, and mother. She is author of *Parenting in the Present Moment*, the *Mindful Parenting* blogger for www.psychcentral.com, and contributing editor at www.kveller.com.

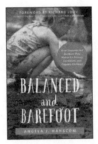

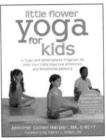